W9-CCN-945

Countdown to College:

21
'To-Do' Lists
for
High School

Step-by-step strategies
for 9th, 10th, 11th and 12th graders

Valerie Pierce
with
Cheryl Rilly

Front Porch Press

Haslett, Michigan

Countdown to College: 21 'To-Do' Lists for High School

Copyright © 2003

Written by Valerie Pierce with Cheryl Rilly
Page design by Terri Haas-Wittmann and Cheryl Rilly

Some quotes have been edited for clarity and brevity.

Published by Front Porch Press, 1724 Vassar Drive, Lansing, Michigan 48912. Phone (517) 487-9295, Fax (517) 487-0888, E-mail: styler@voyager.net

ISBN 0-9656086-7-0

Printed in The United States of America

First Edition
10 9 8 7 6 5 4 3 2 1

acknowledgements
A special thank you to:

▷ **My daughter, Ashlie**, at the University of Texas, whose high school journey to a competitive college, who forced me to create the original lists.

▷ **My husband David and son Tyler**, who still love and support me, after hearing about this book night and day for the last two years.

▷ **Renee Davis**, who encouraged me to use my lists to help other high school college bound students.

▷ **My original manuscript critics**: Carmen, Hayley and Sharon.

▷ **Mary Blaschke**, my daughters' high school counselor, who never appeared to tire from my questions.

▷ **Cy-Springs parents and faculty** who shared this high school journey.

▷ **Wilson and Watkins parents** who requested my original lists and now spread the value of these 'to do lists' to others.

▷ **To my family and friends** for understanding my passion about this book.

a special acknowledgement...

The heart and soul of this book belongs to the remarkable students who shared their thoughts, feelings and insights. Thanks everyone! It wouldn' t have happened without you!

Alexa Saiz, Alison Armstrong, Allison Sudol, Amanda Day, Amber Farris, Amy Meece, Ashlie Pierce, Becca Hall, Bonnie Plott, Brooke Clinton, Cassie Lawin, Catherine Osterman, Chris McMurtry, Clayton Farris, Courtney Chayes, Courtney Kurdziel, Diana Chan, Elizabeth Roman, Erica Kraus, Erika Sjoerdsma, Erin Sprague, Erin Weber, Eugenie Flash, Eva Davison, Fakhri Kalolwala, Garrick Malone, Holly Davidson, Jackie Forinash, Jamie Arredondo, Jason Midgett. Jenna Johansson, Jenni Manion, Jennifer Hassig, Jessica Shepherd, Jill Goodwin, John Holden, Jonathon Koller, Jordan Black, Joyce Jauer, Julie Calvert, Julie Christ, Justice Hampton, Kara Johnson, Kate Hansen, Katherine Schneider, Katie Rhodes, Katrina Bielawski, Ladd Williams, Lindsey Kallsen, Marcus Williams, Marie Falcone, Mary Steffel, Matt Japinga, Matt Klepac, Meaghan Casey, Meghan Miller, Melissa Bohlig, Melissa Lowery, Nicole Mitchell, Niesha Small, Philip Wells, Rebekah Hendrix, Robbie Simon, Robyn Gomez, Roohy Gupta, Sara Waterman, Sarah Dicello, Sheryl Franknecht, Siobhan Malone, Steve Song, Tania Yusaf, Tapas Nuwal, Tiffany Clark, Virginia Smith and William Solomon

Also a special note of gratitude to Jessica Rilly who became our high school freshman guinea pig. Thanks Jess!

table of contents

foreword

The race to the finish line—college, that is—began without our knowledge— when my daughter, Ashlie, entered the 9th grade. From the beginning our biggest problem was knowing what needed to be done before the deadlines passed. Ashlie's extra-curricular commitments, club meetings during homeroom, and trips to the orthodontist caused her to miss information on class meetings and deadlines. More often than not, I'd find student bulletins and parent meeting announcements in the backseat of the car, the floor of her bedroom, or in the trash pile of papers on the kitchen counter.

It didn't get better. Ashlie's activities increased: driver's ed, community service, SAT and ACT testing, evening high school and sports activities, and, oh, yes, schoolwork. To add to the confusion, there was a sudden onslaught of product information and college prep services all touting their own must-do-now importance. The only way out was to organize and prioritize. We made checklists for everything! It was the only way to get things done.

Those checklists became the basis of this book. Thanks to the help of my co-author, Cheryl Rilly, those lists have been expanded. We've gathered all the information, web sites, references, and resources you'll need for your own journey to college—and most importantly, a time-line you'll need to get things done.

Our many 'guiding lights' were the high school counselors and college admissions officers who so unselfishly lent us their expertise, wisdom and insider know-how. With that, many thanks to high school counselors Mary Blaschke, Mary Vertrees, John Dunn, Joanna Erdos, and Maggie Miller and to John Barnhill, Director of Admissions, Florida State University, Gordon Stanley, Director of Admissions, Michigan State University, Tim Washburn, Executive Director Admissions and Records, University of Washington, Dr. Frank Ashley III, Director of Admissions, Texas A&M University, David Drushcel, admissions counselor, Mt. Saint Clare College, and Jean Jordan, Admissions Officer, Emory University. And a special thanks to Suzette Tyler, our publisher and former academic advisor, Michigan State University.

Our other 'couldn't-have-done-it-without-them' group are the wonderful high school and college students who shared their experiences, regrets, and successes with us. You'll find their words throughout the book and a list of their names in special acknowledgements.

Whether you're an incoming freshman or a senior on the brink of making those all-important decisions, it's never too early or too late to use the tools in this book to enhance your high school-to-college experience. Just take it one step at a time.

Good Luck!

Valerie Pierce

freshman year
the journey begins

Even if you have no idea where or whether you want to go to college four years from now, the last thing you want is to find out as a senior that you messed up your chances . . . that there were things you could've done along the way that would've made you a 'shoe-in' at the college of your choice. So, not only should you be **thinking** about college, this book tells you what you can be **doing.**

College or not, the next four years are a chance for you to learn a little more about yourself: to try new things, to learn from mistakes, to dream . . . and to open doors.

66 The good thing
about being a freshman is
all of your choices
are in front of you . . .
you just have to
make the right ones. 99

High School Counselor

freshman year

☐ **Meet** with your counselor to go over your 4-year course schedule. Keep her/him updated throughout high school as you make decisions about what colleges and majors you're considering.

☐ **Ask** both counselors and teachers to keep you informed of any special programs or extracurricular activities that are available.

☐ **Make a list** of academic and personal goals. Revise them at least once a year.

☐ **Get to know** teachers so they get to know you. At some point you may need recommendations for summer programs, scholarships and college applications. Watered-down, generalized recommendations don't help.

☐ **Check out** web sites of your 'dream' colleges. What are their admission requirements? Are you taking the right courses? [ALSO check the requirements for any specific majors you're considering at that school . . . note how much math, science and foreign language is required.]

☐ **Register** at a college web service sites (page 35). Along with access to information on the site, you may be put on mailing lists for other important college material.

☐ **Read** newspapers, bulletin boards, even junk mail! Keep your eyes open for cool activities or opportunities such as: summer programs, camps, academic or sport contests, jobs, or volunteering.

☐ **Create** a file. Get a milk crate and some folders —it doesn't have to be expensive. Keep all your important papers, grades, magazine articles, scholarship opportunities . . . whatever.

☐ **Start** your scholarship search. Yep, it's not too soon (page 19).

☐ **Find** fun and interesting ways to volunteer (page 13).

☐ **Start** a log/journal/portfolio, whatever you want to call it, so that you can keep track of your activities, volunteer work, jobs, and who the contact person is. Write down your impressions, especially what you do and don't like about each activity. Gradually, you may begin to see where your interests—and college major—lie (page 16).

☐ **Talk** with your parents about how much money may be available for your college education. Not a lot? No problem IF you plan ahead (page 91).

66 I won the school Biology Award
and had become really excited
about medicine rather than engineering . . .
BUT I guess I never bothered to tell my
counselor that so he never bothered to tell me
about a program where high school seniors are
GUARANTEED
admission to medical school.
I don't even like to THINK about it . . . 99

Senior, Michigan State U.

let 'em know
who you are . . .

All kinds of cool stuff comes across high school counselors's desks—awards, contests, scholarships, special programs, leadership opportunities, camps . . . **Any one of them could have your name on it** if your counselor has gotten to know you and what your interests and goals are. *It's up to you to make sure he or she does.*

You'll also want to make sure your counselor recognizes why you are a good candidate for the college of your choice. If an admissions officer calls to discuss your application—often the case in borderline situations—your counselor needs to be as convinced as you are that you're a 'good fit'.

mapping out
your 4-year plan

Recommended courses for college:
(Specific requirements vary from college to college. Check with the college you're interested in.)

English: 4* years
literature, language usage, writing (with research paper)
*Including 1/2 year of Speech

Science: 3* years
biology, physical science,
*1 lab strongly recommended

Math: 3-4* years
including intermediate algebra
*4 years strongly recommended

Computers: 1 year
hands-on experience

Social Sciences: 3 years
US and World History

Foreign Language:
3 years
Strongly recommended

Fine/performing arts:
2 years recommended

are 'honors' courses
for you? It depends...

What type of college do you want to attend? Many selective schools give Honors and Advance Placement (AP) grades more weight because they want students who are willing to challenge themselves. So, a 3.5 in Honors English is worth more than a 4.0 in a regular class. The Top 50 Colleges *expect* you to do the maximum amount of work available to you.

On the other hand, there are many less selective schools that don't even take note of honors courses.

What kind of student are you? You DO want to challenge yourself in the courses in which you're strong, BUT you don't want to bury yourself or your GPA. If you think you can get a reasonable grade and your excited about the coursework or the teacher, go for it.

66 I NEVER should've dropped
French my senior year!
I totally blew the college placement test...
I'd forgotten everything! 99

Junior, U. of Georgia

timing IS everything

Set up your schedule so that your senior year includes the courses you'll need to continue as a college freshman. For example, if you're taking 3 years of a language, start in your sophomore year so you'll be 'fresh' for college language courses, or even test out of them altogether.

As for math, take all 4 years even if it doesn't 'agree' with you. That may be all you need to meet basic college requirements and/or you'll be better prepared to 'test out' of it. It's easier to 'gut it out' in high school than in college . . . ask any college freshman.

what colleges are looking for . . .

(ranked by importance)

1. GPA/Class Rank

2. SAT/ACT score

3. Extracurricular activities

Your essays

Teacher/counselor recommendations

66 ...all of a sudden I'm in college
and need to pick up a major.
I wish I'd been more
'involved' in high school
...or worked or done something
that maybe would've given me
an idea of what I like,
what I'm good at...
It's scary not to know. 99

Freshman, Arizona State U.

it's
all about you

you . . . who?

What do you like? If you could do anything, become anything, what would it be? Sure, high school is about learning and preparing for college, but it's also a time to find out about yourself—to become your own person, to think your own thoughts. To do that, you have to draw on your experiences. But, first you have to get them. The more experiences you have and the more you try different things, the more you'll know about yourself.

that's interesting . . .

Colleges want a well-rounded student who's interested and interesting. So, get involved. As a freshman, try a little of everything. As a sophomore and junior, concentrate on 2 or 3 things you really enjoy. That allows you to grow from a member (a joiner), to sitting on a committee (a team player), to heading a committee or holding office (a leader). It also gives the college an idea of what you'll do when you're on campus.

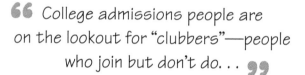

66 College admissions people are on the lookout for "clubbers"—people who join but don't do. . . 99

Admissions Guru,
www.mycollegeguide.org

66 I tried to do it all:
student council, sports, drama, clubs, music. I finally realized that being interested in just a few things is more rewarding. Give your time to things you really love to do—not what you think you have to do. 99

Freshman, George Washington U.

it's all about you

- [ ] **Be a sport.** Try team sports or start a power walking group. Join a yoga class. Too strenuous? Join the pep club or ask the coach if you can film games, manage equipment, or be a student trainer..

- [ ] **Join a club** or start a club—whether it's academic (science, computers) or professional (Future Teachers, Junior Achievement) or social (chess, euchre). Participate in competitions and fairs.

- [ ] **Go political.** Run for student government or work on someone's campaign. Find a cause that interests you and collect signatures for a petition. Help raise funds. Join the debate team.

- [ ] **Work** on the school newspaper, the yearbook, or the school web site. Be a writer, photographer or even a webmaster!

- [ ] **Lend a hand.** Help with school activities, work on fundraisers, build floats, decorate for dances, or plan events.

- [ ] **Get cultured!** Join the band or choir. Act in a school play or join a community theater group. Can't act? Paint scenery, sell tickets, be an usher. Write poetry and read it at a coffee house. Take art or craft lessons.

☐ **Travel** - long trips, short trips, day trips - every chance you get (page 80).

☐ **Volunteer.** Find a great position (page 13).

☐ **Get a hobby.** Check out hobby shops, craft stores and the internet for something interesting. Already have one? Search the internet for related organizations and activities.

☐ **Find a pursuit.** What's special about your heritage or where you live that makes you want to know more?

☐ **Set a goal.** Train for an event. Learn a new instrument. Audition for a play, a band, a commercial! Get certified as a lifeguard.

why volunteer?

a.k.a. 'chalking up points'

Okay, so maybe it *is* because you're such a caring person and not that your high school has a community service requirement or you need N.H.S. points. But don't pat yourself on the back too hard because chances are you'll get as much—or more —out of volunteering as the people you're helping. Not only will admissions folks be impressed but it's one more way for you to learn about YOU—what you do and don't enjoy, what you're good at, and maybe even what you'd like to do some day. Nothing beats a close-up look at what a job involves or meeting people who may be good contacts later. You may even get a lead on scholarships, a summer job, or an internship—not to mention, add to your people skills.

help yourself . . .

Find a volunteer activity that interests you and while you're there, check out the career possibilities. Or, work backwards. Got an idea of what career you'd like to have? Get a volunteer position in a related area. Then talk to people who have the job you want. Look around and find out if you'd be happy. For instance,

If you like:	Then:
Architecture:	→ Build a house with Habitat for Humanity.
Forestry:	→ Be a guide at a state park.
Social Work:	→ Work at a soup kitchen.
Vet Medicine:	→ Help out at an animal shelter.
Ecology:	→ Work at a wildlife sanctuary.
Medicine:	→ Hospitals always need volunteers. Call one.
Music:	→ Work for a radio station's charity event.
Education:	→ Help with an after school program.
Computers:	→ Set up e-mail accounts for seniors in retirement centers.
History:	→ Be a museum guide.
Political Science:	→ Work on a campaign or cause.
Law:	→ Serve at a legal aid center.
Math:	→ Tutor younger kids in your school district.

. . . build your network

You'll meet a lot of people, many of whom you may be able to use as contacts in the admissions process and throughout life. **Get an address book to keep names, phone numbers, and e-mail addresses.**

www.volunteer

Help plant a memorial garden, read to the blind, work on a hotline, do crafts with kids, raise funds, tutor younger kids, collect toys for Christmas. Find opportunities like these and more in your own state at the following sites. They offer a variety of experiences and even tell you how to start your own volunteer program.

www.idealist.org

www.volunteermatch.org

www.cares.org/national

www.servenet.org

the back door . . .

The Back-Door Guide To Short-Term Job Adventures by Michael Landes is a great source for volunteer work, internships, and summer jobs. Read the book and check out the web site for tips and updates:

www.backdoorjobs.com

go global

Any volunteer work you're doing locally can be done nationally or worldwide. In your junior and senior years, instead of working at a local park, contact the U.S. Forest Service and volunteer at a national park. Future architects can contact the U.S. Army Corp of Engineers. Summer programs worldwide need budding social workers. Contact your place of worship for missionary work that can take you into your own backyard or to another country. Many organizations are happy to pick up your expenses in exchange for your helping hand (Travel, page 80).

'quickies' that count

'Event volunteering' and 'virtual volunteering' are two ways to get in your service hours if time or transportation is a problem. Your services are required for a one day event or done via computer. For a schedule of volunteer events and virtual opportunities go to:

www.networkforgood.org

log and learn

Your hours and efforts won't count towards any requirement, unless you document them. Make sure you get verification of your activities from the volunteer organization. Or, make your own log. Along with your name, the contact person's name and telephone number, the date, the activity and how many hours you spent, leave room to write what you liked and what you didn't like. Ask yourself these questions and include your thoughts:

- **What did I learn?**
- **What impressed me or suprised me the most?**
- **What was a total turn off?**
- **Did the activity leave me feeling good? Overwhelmed? Disinterested?**
- **What careers did I find out about?**
- **Do I want to learn more about it?**
- **Could I imagine doing this kind of work for life?**

volunteering

☐ **List** your interests and match them to possible service opportunities.

☐ **Call** professional organizations and associations related to your interests to see if they need volunteers or could suggest a volunteer position.

☐ **Click on** the web sites (page 15) for ideas. In your junior and senior years, check the sites for out-of-state opportunities.

☐ **Check** the school bulletin board or with your counselor to see what service possibilities exist through your school.

☐ **Ask** your friends where they plan to volunteer.

☐ **Check** the web sites of local newspapers and televison station for lists of volunteer activites and events. Watch for stories on interesting charity events. Call the sponsoring agency and ask if you can volunteer.

☐ **Call** the local sports teams to see if they're sponsoring youth events. Ask if you can volunteer.

☐ **Check** with your place of worship. Can you teach Sunday school? Baby sit? Volunteer at church events? Do they sponsor missionary work?

☐ **Turn** your interests into volunteer work. If you take extracurricular classes (i.e. dance, music), ask if they need help.

☐ **Start** your own volunteer group - form a 'zoo crew,' adopt a highway mile or adapt a program to suit your community.

TO HELP YOURSELF . . .

☐ **Be curious.** Find out what careers are related to the volunteer situation (i.e. hospital: doctor, nurse, radiologist, physical therapist, etc).

☐ **Talk** to your supervisor. Find out if your volunteer position can turn into a summer job or internship. Ask if he/she knows any programs or scholarships that could benefit you.

☐ **Use** your summer volunteer work to travel. Check with your place of worship for mission trips. Call the national headquarters of local organizations for out-of-state possibilities. Check the volunteer web sites for national or worldwide opportunities.

☐ **Create** a volunteer log or form letter to document your hours. Attach notes to your log about what you liked or disliked about a volunteer experience.

☐ **Ask** your counselor if your school has a program that gives high school credit for community service hours.

get
scholarships

you don't have
to be Einstein . . .

. . . or a jock to get scholarships, but
you do have to be detective. Finding scholarships
is like a game of 'Where's Waldo?' There are
scholarships for everything—bagpipe players,
people under four feet tall, anyone who wants to
study parapsychology or young women who want
to become engineers. Start looking now because
it takes time! Besides, it 'pays' to plan ahead.
Some clubs and volunteer organizations give
scholarships to members and workers. So, why
not put your community service hours and extracurricular time into an organization that ultimately
may help you?

MY MAMA'S A TRUCK DRIVER

Great! Then she's probably a union member and most unions offer scholarships to family members. What you and your family do, where they work and shop all point to scholarship money. Check out this profile and then create your own. Include aunts, uncles, grandparents, cousins—the companies they work for and organizations they belong to. Then dig up your ancestors. What's your heritage? Ethnicity? Write down everything that makes you YOU.

Joe's scholarship leads include:

Businesses:	Associations:
Coca-Cola	Naval Reserve
Wheaties	Lion`s Club
Doublemint	Eagle Scouts
Tylenol	Luthern Brotherhood
Calgon	Junior Achievement
Wal-Mart	Electricians union
Target	Engineering society
McDonald's	Teachers' association
Exxon	
Mastercard & Visa	

Contests:
Intel Science Talent Search
Baush & Lomb Science Award

Miscellaneous:
National Merit Scholarship
Texas A & M scholarships for sports, music, etc.
Sam Walton Community Scholarship
Polish/Slavic-related organizations

Who's Joe?

. . . a profile

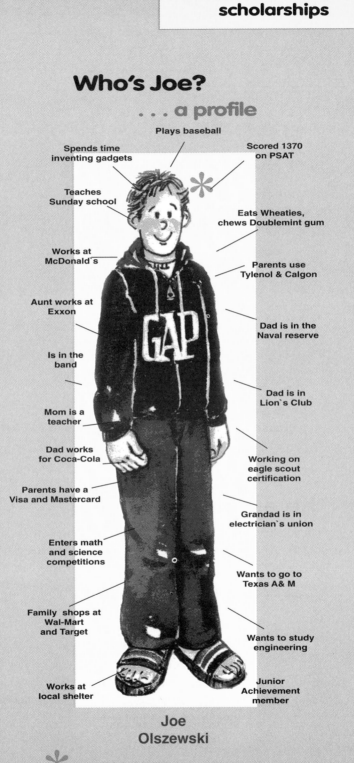

Plays baseball

Spends time inventing gadgets

Scored 1370 on PSAT

Teaches Sunday school

Eats Wheaties, chews Doublemint gum

Works at McDonald's

Parents use Tylenol & Calgon

Aunt works at Exxon

Dad is in the Naval reserve

Is in the band

Dad is in Lion's Club

Mom is a teacher

Dad works for Coca-Cola

Working on eagle scout certification

Parents have a Visa and Mastercard

Grandad is in electrician's union

Enters math and science competitions

Wants to go to Texas A& M

Family shops at Wal-Mart and Target

Wants to study engineering

Works at local shelter

Junior Achievement member

Joe Olszewski

*Joe is an entirely fictional student with far too many activities to be real. He's here only to show you how many possibilities exist. No one expects you to be 'super student'. Do not try this at home.

show me the
money!

Start your scholarship search at:

- **Libraries and bookstores.** Books such as College Board Scholarship Handbook come with a CD-ROM so you can view them via computer.

- **Your high school's college and career center** has scholarship books and may even have a scholarship database.

- **Your counselor** knows about many local scholarships. Show him/her the profile you've written and he/she may be able to suggest more.

- **Local businesses and organizations.** Call and ask if they sponsor scholarships, awards, or contests.

And . . .

the e-search

Scholarship search web sites speed up your research. Register with as many as possible and choose the broadest criteria for the most leads. The information will overlap but each site has one or two different listings that may be worth it.

www.finaid.org

www.fastweb.com

www.collegeboard.com

www.scholarship.com

www.review.com

www.srnexpress.com

www.xap.com

www.wiredscholar.com

www.eduprep.com

www.allaboutcollege.com

66 Senior year is the time to APPLY for scholarships, not LOOK for them . . . You don't have time! 99

Sophomore, U. of Texas

In 10th, 11th and 12th grade

update your Internet searches and scan the books again. Check with the guidance office for any leads on local and national scholarships. Talk to seniors and find out what scholarships they qualified for, especially local scholarships.

When you start getting serious about what colleges are in the running, check out their web sites for scholarships available through them. Talk to the Financial Aid Officer and ask for leads. If you know what your major will be, call the departments at the colleges and ask if they know of any scholarships.

Get good at looking for scholarships. Once you're in college, there are more you can apply for every year—especially in your major.

never pay anyone to search for scholarships for you . . .

They'll only take the same information, plug it into the same sites and get the same results.

For information on scholarship scams go to:

www.fraud.org

www.ftc.gov.bcp/conline/edcams/scholarship

it's never too early to hear
ka-ching!

Don't wait until you're a senior to cash in.
There's money available as early as your freshman year. In addition to scholarships, there are CONTESTS! Even if you don't enter anything as a freshman, knowing what's out there now will help you decide what to go after later. The list below will give you an idea of what's out there starting in the 9th grade.

American Legion Oratorical Contest	→ $1,500 - $18,000
Ayn Rand Essay Contests	→ $1,000
The DuPont Challenge	→ $50 - $1,500
Duracell/NTSA Invention Challenge	→ $500 - $20,000
National History Day Contest	→ $250 - $1,000
National Peace Essay Contest	→ $1,000 -$10,000
Prudential Spirit of Community Awards	→ $1,000 - $5,000
Scholastic Art and Writing Awards	→ $100 - $1,000
ThinkQuest Internet Challenge	→ $3,000 - $25,000
Toshiba/NSTA ExploraVision Awards	→ $100 - $10,000
Young Naturalist Awards	→ $1,000
Young America Creative Patriotic Art Awards	→ $500 - $3,000

Information compiled from: **How To Go To College Almost For Free**, *Ben Kaplan.*

. . . mining for money
How To Go To College Almost For Free

was written by Ben Kaplan, a one-time

public school student who wanted to attend

Harvard. His problem: no money. His solution:

scholarships, nearly $90,000 worth. He put his

tips and strategies into the book, a MUST read.

scholarships

YEARLY TO-DO'S:

☐ **First things first**—start a file for scholarships, awards, and contests. Keep adding and updating it yearly.

☐ **Search the sites.** Register at the web sites (page 22). Update your listing at least yearly or when your GPA and class rank change.

☐ **Check** out the scholarship section at the library and bookstores.

☐ **Enter** contests. Ask your counselor and teachers what programs they know of and check out *The Scholarhip Scouting Report* by Ben Kaplan.

☐ **Check** out who won. Go to the scholarship's web site. The winning essay or portfolio is usually available. Study it for tips.

☐ **Get extra credit.** Check if you can use scholarship essays or projects as a school assignment or an extra credit project.

☐ **Keep** your counselor informed about your interests. He/she may know of related scholarships.

FRESHMAN YEAR:

☐ **Check** volunteer agencies to see which ones give volunteer scholarships. Consider doing your community service hours there.

☐ **Join** clubs that give scholarships to members. Do this early. Most clubs require at least a one year membership for eligibility.

☐ **Write** your profile to see what scholarship opportunities exist (page 20). List where you and your parents shop, bank, buy gas, and have your utilities. Put them on your list of organizations to contact.

SOPHOMORE YEAR:

☐ **Update** your internet searches.

☐ **Check** with the guidance office for local scholarships that are available and what their requirements are.

☐ **List** local businesses, organizations and clubs. Contact them to see if they offer scholarships or contests.

☐ **Check** with any associations and organizations you, your parents, or extended family members belong to for scholarships and contests.

JUNIOR YEAR:

☐ **Study** for the PSAT. Taking it makes you eligible for the National Merit Scholarships (page 46).

☐ **Talk** to seniors to find out what scholarships they're applying for, especially local ones. Ask them about scholarships offered through their colleges.

☐ **Send** for applications as soon as possible. Keep an eye on deadlines and requirements.

☐ **Pick** up local scholarship applications that are available from your guidance office. Get them before the school year ends so you can work on the application and required essay during summer.

☐ **Contact** the athletic department at your selected colleges to apply for sports scholarships (page 82). Do this during the summer. It doesn't matter if you decide NOT to attend a particular college. You can always decline an offer.

SENIOR YEAR:

☐ **Contact** the financial aid counselors at your selected colleges to see what scholarships they have. If you know your major, check with that department to see what scholarships they know are available. Scholarships differ from college to college. This may even be a deciding factor in your final college choice (pages 98 and 135).

☐ **Watch** the deadlines. Most applications are due in February but some have deadlines as early as fall.

☐ **Keep** applying. Check to see if any essay you've written can be used for more than one award. Be careful not to get carried away with this—you might waste time and lose money.

☐ **Follow** the directions of the application to the letter. Omitting information can disqualify you.

☐ **Ask** for letters of recommendation early. Allow ample time for your teachers and employers to write and send them. Follow up to make sure they're sent in on time. Also ask for one copy of the letter that doesn't refer to a specific scholarship so that if another scholarship comes up, you may use the same recommendation.

☐ **Notify** the college you've decided to attend of scholarships you'll be receiving.

66 I ended up with a 'full ride'
—tuition and housing—
just for being a caddy!
Not bad for helping people
chase a little white ball . . .* 99

Senior, Ohio State U.

*An Evans Scholarship

10

(very cool) things to make your summers count

using your 'free spins'

Summer vacations, long weekends, and winter and spring breaks are 'free spins' in the game of preparing for college. You can sneak in all kinds of stuff—visit campuses, get ahead of required reading, learn new skills, explore careers and majors, earn high school *AND* college credit, make a little money, find a little money, get your community service hours in, prepare for college testing, expand your view of the world—or just contemplate your navel and use the time to discover yourself. Do you have to do *all* of them? NO! Go at your own pace. . .even if you do one or two things every summer, you're way ahead of the game.

head for the campus

Programs & Camps?
How about . . .
Film making
Fencing
Kayaking
Gold panning
Entomology
Pre-Law
Pre-Med
Rappelling
Blacksmithing
Make-up
Bird watching
Model rockets
Glacier travel
African languages
Drum majoring
White water rafting
Dog sledding
Circus arts
Journalism
Time management
Ice climbing
Adventure racing
Music
Engineering
Golf
did we mention . . .
Football, dance &
web page design?

Almost every college in the U.S. offers fantastic summer programs for high school students. What's your choice? Sports? The arts? Academics? Computer science? They offer great learning experiences and you're able to get a 'feel' for college.

Call local colleges or any others you'd like to 'try on' to see what they offer. Check with your school's guidance office, bulletin boards, and web site for any program they may be hosting or know about. Professional organizations also host campus programs. If there's a field you're interested in, contact the related professional organization to see what they offer and where it's located.

66 Exposure is everything for high school athletes. If you have a particular college you're interested in, go to their summer sports camp. The coaching staff notices kids who excel. 99

Assistant Coach,. Eastern Michigan U.

Most programs are available to sophomores and up. But look over the possibilities *NOW*. Deadlines are usually in March. You'll need an application and a recommendation from a teacher, counselor, administrator or coach— and plenty of time to decide which camp to attend. For a listing of over 3000 camps, go to:

www.petersons.com/summerop/

Check out these books for even more programs:

Summer Opportunities for Kids & Teenagers
(Petersons)

Kaplan Yale Daily News Guide to Summer Programs
(Yale Daily News)

Summer on Campus
(Shirley Levin)

psssst . . .

Can't afford the programs and camps?
Don't count them out. It's not publicized but financial aid is usually available. If you want to attend, call 'em! Ask for aid. The earlier you apply to ANY program, the better your chances are, especially if aid is involved. Don't wait!

summer camps

Day camps, away camps, supercamps—they're all great places to learn new skills. Look for camps that teach computer or leadership skills, speed reading, time management, sports, art, or anything that interests you. Check with your counselor for camps in your area or for a list of camps, go to:

www.acacamps.org
www.supercamp.com

we're telling you now . . .

During the summer there are numerous opportunities to develop leadership skills—camps, institutes, conferences, workshops—often on college campuses. For a few, such as Boys' State and Girls' State, you must be selected → → by your principal or counselor, while most are open to all. Check with your counselor to see what is availble and if you are interested, let them know.

go to school

Riiiight . . . just what you wanted to do. But it really is a good time to take one course—in the classroom or on-line. Take something difficult and you can give it your full attention . . . or get rid of a Physical Education requirement and free up an hour during the school year so you can take another course. If you're a junior or senior, you may want to take a course at a local college so you can get 'dual credit' (page 115). A word of caution—check with both your high school and any college you're considering to confirm which courses are accepted and for how many credits.

make some bucks

Too young to get a traditional job? Become self-employed. Get training to become a lifeguard, caddy at the golf course, detail cars, cut grass, baby sit, walk dogs, paint houses. In your junior and senior years, get a part-time job or an internship related to the field you may be interested in pursuing.

For Boys State go to:

www.legion.org

For Girls State go to:

www.legion-aux.org

read

During the summer before your sophomore and junior year, get the reading list for the next school year. When you're a senior, read for college. Contact the English departments at the colleges you're considering or check their web sites for required reading lists. Start with books that are common to all the lists. For a general college book list pick up *Reading Lists for College Bound Students* by Doug Estell—or go to:

www.ala.org/yalsa/

www.collegeboard.com/plan_ning/themost/

booklist.html

❝ There was a great summer program I was dying to go to so I asked the Rotary Club if they would pay for it in exchange for me making a presentation to their group after I returned. They were, and I did. They were so impressed, they gave me scholarship money for college. ❞

Freshman, Albion College

33

visit colleges

Start with walk-throughs just to get the feel of a campus. Check out the activities and go to a play or a game. Hang out. And while you're wandering among the students, imagine yourself on campus in a few years. Save the in-depth visits for your junior and senior years. Don't forget virtual tours on the Internet—all colleges have 'em (page 68).

> **❝** Going to a math and science summer camp sounded geeky, but it turned out to be pretty cool. We stayed in the dorms so not only did I get a 'feel' for college life, I'm 'aceing' math this year . . . I used to hate it! **❞**
>
> Sophomore, East Kentwood High School

travel

Vacation with your parents and visit a college town. Attend an out-of-state (or at least out-of-your-area) summer program on a college campus or at a camp. Check with your place of worship for any summer missions they may be hosting. Or, do day trips with youth groups. Don't forget to check with the volunteer web sites (page 15) for out-of-state possibilities and see 'Travel' (page 80) for more opportunities.

search for scholarships

Forget the Play Station for a few minutes and register at a scholarship search site (page 22). Check with your local library to see if they have a scholarship database or if your high school is willing, use theirs. Hit the bookstores and library for scholarship books. During the summer before your senior year, send for scholarship applications, work on your essays, get teacher recommendations, and put necessary portfolios together.

Register with college prep web sites. They're loaded with scholarship info as well as discussion boards, test preps and all kinds of college advice.

www.plansforme.com

www.review.com

www.students.gov

www.teenink.com

www.allaboutcollege.com

www.mapping-your-future.org

www.collegeispossible .org

volunteer

Get your community service hours in now and you'll free up your time during the school year. Feeling ambitious? Start your own do-good group or propose a program to an organization you're working with already. Like what you're doing? Ask if you can come back next year as an intern or if a paid job will be available.

ok ladies . . .

One of the best things that ever happened to female college students is **'Title IX'—the rule that makes colleges set aside money for women's sports.** Want a scholarship? Then use your summers to improve your skills in a sport: golf, tennis, volleyball, field hockey. . .The least you'll get out of it is being healthy.

test prep

Start preparing for the PSAT, PLAN, SAT, ACT and SAT II tests (page 46 and 83). Find out if your high school or school district offers a summer prep program or look for a summer camp that offers classes. Take the sample tests at the testing organizations' web sites or check out the library and bookstores for prep books.

learn to . . .

66 SPEEDREAD.
You either read fast
in college or get left behind. 99

Freshman, U of Houston.

66 TYPE. PROPERLY.
Hunting and pecking just slows you down
too much, especially if you're trying
to take notes in class. 99

Freshman, U of Wisconsin.

make your summers count

YEARLY TO-DO'S:

☐ **Call** colleges to find out what types of summer programs they offer.

☐ **Check** with your school's guidance office, bulletin board and web site for summer programs they're hosting or may know about.

☐ **Explore** web sites and books (page 31) for college summer programs. Look for ones related to your interests, ones that teach skills (i.e. computer training), or are just too fun to pass up.

☐ **Call** professional organizations related to your interests for programs they may offer.

☐ **Check** with sport associations (local, national, minor, and professional) for camps and programs. Join or volunteer your services.

☐ **Apply** to programs and camps early. Get in the habit of looking now for programs to attend next year.

☐ **Ask** the program your interested in for financial aid, if you need it.

☐ **Sign up** for a class—on-line or in the classroom.

☐ **Make money.** Save money. Be creative and start your own business or get a summer job.

☐ **Volunteer.** If your high school has a program that gives credit for community service hours, arrange your volunteer hours to get that credit.

☐ **Update** your log. Make note of whatever program or camp you attend, your volunteer work, any summer jobs, extra classes, skills, or travel.

SUMMER BEFORE SOPHOMORE YEAR:

☐ **Get** the reading list for your sophomore year. Polish off at least one book.

☐ **Walk** around a local college campus. Explore campuses nationwide with "virtual tours" (page 68).

☐ **Start** your scholarship search if you haven't already. Sign up at the search sites (page 22).

☐ **Travel.** Ask if your family vacation can include a stop at a college town. If you belong to a youth or church group, check if they're planning any trips—whether it's for the day, a weekend, or longer.

SUMMER BEFORE JR & SR YEAR:

☐ **Look** for summer programs held on the campuses of colleges you're considering. (Remember to express your hopes of attending that college to faculty members.)

☐ **Take** either a high school class or a 'dual credit' class (page 115). Ask your counselor what class is best for you.

☐ **Get** a job related to the major you'd like to study in college.

☐ **Read** at least one book from next year's reading list.

☐ **Begin** your serious visits to the colleges you're considering (page 63).

☐ **Update** your scholarship search with your current GPA and class rank.

☐ **Work** on your scholarship and college application essays during the summer before your senior year (page 105).

☐ **Prepare** for the PSAT (page 46), the SAT, ACT, and SAT II tests (page 83).

☐ **Find** opportunities to travel—whether it's volunteering, studying out-of-state or overseas (page 80), or vacationing with your family.

66 I didn't have a clue
what college I wanted to
go to . . . I just took challenging
courses and got good grades
which kept my options open
until I figured it out.
That worked for me . . . 99

Freshman, Tulane U.

10

sophomore year
keep on keepin' on

The best way to get where you want to go is to set goals . . . whether it's better grades, getting into your dream college, playing a sport, or whatever. Just deciding what's important to you in the long run will help you focus on what you have to do now. Break it down...what is it that you want to accomplish in your sophomore year? The first semester? The first week? What's it take to make that happen? Keep setting goals and revise them as you go. You'll not only get what you want but also gain the confidence of knowing you're capable of just about anything you set your mind to.

sophomore year

☐ **Sign** up in September for the PSAT (page 45). This one's practice... the real one is Junior year. Consider taking the PLAN.

☐ **Focus** on your GPA. Take the most challenging classes you can handle.

☐ **Narrow** down your activities to two or three that you'll do throughout high school and may pursue in college.

☐ **Start** a list of colleges to consider. Be sure to go to any college fairs in your area... you'll learn the 'language' of exploring colleges. Use virtual tours and begin thinking about which colleges you'd like to visit in-depth (page 63).

☐ **Take** the personality/interest inventory tests on page 48 if you need help determining colleges or majors. Or, do it just for fun. They ask the questions you need to be asking yourself.

☐ **Plan** your summer. Find programs and camps to attend. Check with your counselor to decide if a summer class is appropriate (page 29).

☐ **Continue** your scholarship search (page 19).

sophomore basics

☐ **Review** for the PSAT, SAT and ACT during the summer (pages 45 and 83).

☐ **Update** your records of activities, volunteer work, programs, classes, and traveling. File information you receive on colleges, scholarships and tests.

☐ **Review** and revise your goals . . . set new ones.

☐ **Think** careers! Talk to people about their jobs (page 51).

. . . **homework helper**

Stuck? Got an algebra problem that's impossible? Don't understand the symbolism of a book? Science class leaving you dazed and confused? Check out the homework help sites before you need them, so you know which one works best for you: **www.bigchalk.com**

www.gomath.com

43

❝ Everyone says that
the key to success in school
is 'getting organized.'
I disagree . . .
It's staying organized! **❞**

Senior, Salem High School

the tests:
psat & plan

sneak previews

Relaaaax! The tests you can take this year are important but they won't affect your college admission. So, why take them? Two reasons. You'll find out what your academic strengths and weaknesses are (while you can still do something about it) and **because you can.** Any time you get a chance to try something out before it counts—whether it's a test, volunteering to see if you like a major or a career, or taking a program on a campus of a college you're considering attending—*DO IT!*

the

The SAT"s baby brother

PSAT

Preliminary Scholastic Assessment Test

The PSAT is given to students in October of their *Junior* year. *It's your option to take it this year.*

why should you take it in your sophomore year?

- **You can totally blow it** and it doesn't count. *Only the junior year PSAT score is used as criteria* for some scholarships (notably the National Merit Scholarship). Next year when it does count, you'll know what to expect.

- **You'll find out what your strengths and weaknesses are.** Your scores (sent in December) will clue you in to subjects and skills you need to focus on.

- **You'll get mail.** Colleges will begin to send you information on their schools and programs. You'll get an early jump on what's out there.

- **Actual SAT questions are included** in the PSAT. You'll begin to familiarize yourself with that test, too.

. . . good for you . . . but

You took the PSAT this year and scored well? Good for you. BUT...you still have to take it again in your junior year to be eligible for scholarships.

the
PLAN
The ACT's baby brother
The pre-American College Test (ACT)

what is it?

- **PLAN** is the pre-American College Test. If your school offers it, you'll take it as a sophomore. (PLAN is not used for scholarships.)

- **Your academic strength and weakness** are identified with this test, too. With your counselors and teachers you can use the results to help plan your coursework for the rest of high school. For the test to really work for you, get the test book back and review what questions you 'blew' and why. If it was quadratic equations, then you know exactly where you need to focus your efforts.

the problem is . . .

Not every school gives this test. Since it's the sneak preview of the ACT, if you don't take it, you lose the chance to see what the ACT is like.

The solution: Ask your counselor to find a school that's giving PLAN and go! If you can't find one, ACT will send a test for you to be taken at your school. The cost is under $10.

to find out more...

about the PSAT and PLAN, visit the test companies' web sites:

(PSAT & SAT)
www.collegeboard.com

(PLAN)
www.act.org

47

'psych' yourself out!
online personality test to find. . .

. . . the right college . . .

www.usnews.com/usnews/edu/
college/tools/brief/cpq/coquiz.htm

The *US News and World Report* site offers a *College Personality Quiz* that identifies the type of colleges where you'd most likely feel comfortable and do well. Links to the colleges, virtual tours and more info are available.

www.review.com

This *Princeton Review* site offers 10th and 11th graders a *Complete Student Match* to help find a college. It also has a *Career Assessment Quiz* but this one will cost you (under $50). Still . . . it's a great site for tips and information.

. . . the right major . . .

www.allthetests.com

www.testingroom.com

There's an entire battery of career and personality tests that will allow you to zero in on your interests and possible majors. Take one, take 'em all. They're free.

. . . the right career . . .

www.wiredscholar.com/preparing/content/
prep_assess.jsp#person

This personality test can be taken in under two minutes. Immediate results give you a list of careers that fit your personality type.

. . . for you.

August/September:

☐ **Tell** your counselor you want to take the PSAT this year—otherwise it may not be offered to you. Find out the date it will be given and how to register. *Note: Stay on top of this one so your counselor doesn't forget.*

☐ **Ask** about PLAN. If your school doesn't administer it, ask your counselor to find a school that does or make arrangements to have it administered to you at your school.

☐ **Sign** up. Register and pay for the tests through the guidance office.

☐ **Check** the test web sites (page 47) for more information and sample questions.

October:

☐ **Get** the review packet for the PSAT from your counselor at least one week before the test.

☐ **Take** the PSAT and/or PLAN

December:

☐ **Review** your test scores with your counselor. Get your test book back and go over the questions you answered incorrectly. Talk to him/her about how you can improve in these areas.

66 There is no 'magic morning'
when you wake up and
KNOW
what you want to do.
You have to get involved . . .
pay attention to what
interests you . . .
What you're looking for
is a 'FEEL' for what
you really want in life. 99

Junior, Columbia U.

get

a life!

so, waddaya wanna be?

You're only 15 and we're asking you to pick a career?!? Well, no, but we are telling you that you need to get in the habit of talking to people about what they do all day—their jobs! The best way to find out about careers is to talk to the people doing them. How else are you going to find out that your 'dream' job includes a 60 hour work week? Or sleeping in not-so-dreamy motels four months of the year? Or any number of other things you don't want to do? On the other hand, you may get great first-hand information on how to achieve your dream, little known shortcuts, and maybe even wind up with a mentor or an internship.

the only
dumb question...

. . . is the one unasked! Talk to everyone—people you know, people you don't know. The following questions will get you started:

What do you do on a typical day?

What abilities and talents are needed to be successful?

What type of training and education is necessary?

What kind of education and work experiences did you have in order to get this position?

Besides salary and fringe benefits, do you feel rewarded?

Is there a college that you would recommend?

What is the future like for this field? Is there a demand for this position?

If you could do it all over again, would you still want to do what you do?

What kinds of sacrifices and disappointments might I face?

What could I be doing now to prepare for this career?

What professional organizations or journals are there where I could learn more?

Could you give me any advice?

. . . wanna be a rock star?

Read *The Occupational Outlook Handbook...* by the US Department of Labor, it's lots of ink but you'll get the 'nitty gritty' on every job in American—education requirements, salaries, forecasts, and trends. Zero in on the jobs that sound interesting. You can view it on-line or at a library. **www.bis.gov/oco**

to do's
get a life

- [ ] **Talk** with the adults you know. You might hear of a career you never knew existed.

- [ ] **List** the careers you'd like to have and the names of people who have these jobs. Write a letter, e-mail or call the person you want to interview and set up an appointment. *Don't know anyone? Then:*

  - **Call professional organizations** (i.e. Society of Automotive Engineeers). Ask if they could refer you to someone in your area.

    or

  - **Flip through magazines** related to that career (i.e. *Psychology Today*). Look for stories that profile people who have the job you want.

    or

  - **Call the Human Resources Department** of a business and ask if they could refer you to someone in their company.

    or

  - **Talk to people** who work in conjunction with a career. Actors, musicians, writers, and artists have agents and managers who are more accessible than the talent.

- [ ] **Follow up.** Send a handwritten thank you note (*not e-mail!*) after talking with them. Later, contact them to see if they know of any summer programs, jobs, or internships.

☐ **Check** out Career Days. Ask speakers about the college they attended—or wish they had attended.

☐ **Skim** through the books in the career section at your high school or library for jobs that interest you.

☐ **Check** with colleges for major-related summer programs and camps—pre-med, pre-law, computer science, engineering—it's a great way to find out if you like the field AND make great contacts.

☐ **Flip** through a college course catalog for areas of study that seem interesting. Check the prerequisite classes to see if you like them, too.

☐ **Talk** to your counselor if you find a career or field of study that you'd like to pursue. Make sure your classes are on the right track.

... career software programs

Some high schools have **career software programs** available to their students. Plug in your interests, abilities, goals, etc. and you're provided with a variety of appropriate careers, their job descriptions, projected income, availability—and which colleges offer related majors. If your high school has this program—

USE IT!

it's
time to start
'the list'

finding the right colleges . . .

. . . to apply to takes some work.
But there's a better reason to start your search early—**every college has different admission requirements**. That affects how many AP classes you'll need, if any. You'll know how important extracurricular activities are— or aren't. You'll be able to check out course requirements for specific majors **in addition to** the college's required coursework. Start considering colleges now and you'll also have more time to visit campuses, more time to compare schools, more time to find out about financial aid packages, and you'll spend less time second guessing yourelf. **So start your list now.**

college
search sites

College search sites match colleges to your interests and abilities. Play at these sites. Change your preferences just a bit and you'll wind up with an entirely different list which might pop up a college that's perfect for you. Sites differ, so try 'em all:

www.collegeboard.org
www.usnews.com/usnews/edu/college/cohome.htm
www.petersons.com
www.collegeview.com
www.review.com
www.collegeexpress.com
www.xap.com
www.collegenet.com

Think about it . . .

There are over 4,000 four year colleges in the U.S. Add to that about another 1900 community colleges—so how do you decide which schools to consider? Start by deciding what's necessary *for you*.

Academics:
What do you want to study? Do you want a specific major or will a liberal arts degree do? Does your area of study require special facilities?

Location:
Where do you want to live? Big city? Small town? Do yo want to go to the beach every day or turn into a snow bunny during the winter?

Size:
Do you want to be part of a large student body or a small one? Do you want 100 kids in a class or 30?

Distance:
Do you want to stay at home or be close enough to drop your laundry off for mom to do every two weeks? Or move far away?

66 Deciding which university
to attend feels like the most
important decision of your life;
it's not. Take a deep breath and
follow your heart. Every school
has as much to offer as you're
willing to put into it. 99

Freshman, Carnegie Mellon U.

You:
Are you more comfortable in a structured class or are you focused enough to do independent study? Do you want to be academically challenged or prefer to skip the brain drain?

Extracurriculars:
What activites do you want to participate in outside of the classroom? Do you want to join a sorority or fraternity?

Sports:
Do you want to play a sport at college? Does the football team have to be Bowl Game-bound every year?

Reputation:
Do you want to go to a 'party' school? Or one that's known for being highly selective?

$$$$$$$:
What's affordable? If you rely on student loans, is a school that costs more still worthwhile?

Lehigh University
27 Memorial Drive, W.
Bethlehem, PA 18015
(610) 758-3100

US News ranking: Nat. U —
Doc., No. 40

Website: http://www.lehigh.edu

Admissions e-mail:
admissions@lehigh.edu
Private; founded 1865

Setting: Urban

Degrees offered: bachelor's,
master's, doctorate

Calendar: semester

Freshman admission: more selective;
2001-2002: 8,088 applied; 3,776 accepted. Either SAT or ACT required. SAT
25/75 percentile: 1200-1370. High
school rank: 52% in top tenth, 84% in
top quarter, 99% in top half.

Early decision deadline: 11/15
notification date: 12/23 Application
deadline (fall): 1/1 Common application:
yes TOEFL requirement: yes Undergraduate student body: 4,596 full time,
54 part time; 59% male, 41% female; 0%
American Indian, 6% Asian, 3% black,
3% Hispanic, 85% white, 3% international; 31% from in state; 65% live on
campus; 38% of students in fraternities,
43% in sororities.

Most popular majors: 5% finance,
5% mechanical engineering, 4% computer engineering, 4% industrial/manufacturing engineering, 2% psychology.

Class size: 39% have fewer than 20
students; 47% have between 20 and 50
students; 14% have 50 or more students.

Expenses: 2002-2003: Tuition
$26,180; room/board $7,530.

Financial Aid: (610) 758-3181; 58%of
undergrads applied for financial aid; 46%
of undergrads determined to have financial need; average aid package $19, 697;
those receiving need-base aid have 98%
of need met; 72% of undergrads' need
is fully met; 45% of undergrads receive
need-based grants, average grant $15,
146; average student indebtedness at
graduation: $18, 489; 56% of grads with
debt.

from: *US News & World Report, 2003
Edition America's Best Colleges*

must reads

Each year *Newsweek* and
US News and World Report
publish special college
editions. School profiles
and requirements, along
with updates, great advice,
tips, sample tests, college
rankings, and contact information are included:

*US News
and World Report:
America's Best Colleges*

*Newsweek:
How To Get Into
College*

66 If you want to
know what a
college is looking
for in a student,
call the
admissions
department . . .
We always like
to talk to
a customer. 99

**Admissions Counselor,
Mt. Saint Clare College**

pricey schools?
don't count 'em out

Your Expected Family Contribution (EFC)—the amount of tuition your family is expected to pay (page 92)—stays roughly the same no matter how expensive a school is. Schools want a diverse student population and to get that, they may be willing to help you. If you total your federal aid, scholarships and work-study programs, your student loan may be the same as a less expensive school.

very 'selective' schools?
consider counting them out

Sure, 'Ivies' are prestigious, but a study sponsored by the National Bureau of Economic Research showed that middle-class students earned a higher income later on when they attended *a college whose average SAT scores were 1000* as opposed to *a college whose average SAT scores were 1200.* Taking two students who are equal, the student who attends a slightly less selective institution will probably have higher grades, a higher class rank, stand out more to faculty, and have more confidence in his or her abilities.

grades, SATs . . . fuh-ged-about-it!
Want to go to a college that doesn't give grades? How about one that doesn't care about your SAT score? Want to study computer gaming? Design your own degree program? Or go to a school that has a golf course on campus? Read Donald Asher's *Cool Colleges for the Hyper-Intelligent, Self-Directed, Late Blooming, and Just Plain Different.* A great way to find colleges you'd never think of on your own.

59

gurus, coaches & advisors
on-line

The sites below will offer you answers quickly and from a lot of different sources: college advisors, coaches, admissions folks, high school and college students. Check out the bulletin boards, Q & A pages and chat sites.

www.mycollegeguide.org/guru

www.collegeconfidential.com

www.studentscoop.com

www.teenink.com

www.myfootpath.com

'Best of the Best'

www.scholarstuff.com

This site lists colleges in every state in the U.S. with links to their web sites, PLUS links to each college's chat room so you can see what students on campus are talking about, PLUS e-mail addresses to each admissions office—a quick way to request information.

'the list' to do's

☐ **List** what you want in a college (page 56).

☐ **Register** at the college search sites (page 57) to help develop a list of colleges to research. Vary your location, class size, etc. to produce more choices.

☐ **Read** the college editions of *US News and World Report* and *Newsweek* (page 58). Pick up the new edition yearly.

☐ **Add** any schools that may be recommended by family, friends, counselors, teachers, magazines, or books to your list.

Next . . .

☐ **Visit** the college web sites and take a virtual tour of the campuses.

☐ **Register** at the colleges' web sites and request an information pack (you can also call the admissions office for this).

☐ **Call** the admissions office if you have any questions about the requirements.

☐ **Plan** on-campus visits to narrow down your choices further (page 63).

66 Don't rely on the
mood swings of friends . . .
I was considering Notre Dame
until I talked with a buddy
who was a first semester
freshman there . . . He had
NOTHING good to say about the
place! Based on that, *I didn't*
even apply. He now raves about
how great the school is . . . Guess
he got over his 'freshman funk'.
My advice?
Take a formal tour. 99

Sophomore, Indiana U.

the

campus visits

the test drive

You'll want to start visiting colleges the summer before your junior year. Tours with student guides take about an hour or two; but most colleges have programs that allow you to stay overnight in a dorm, sit in on classes, meet with teachers and coaches, and interview with admissions officers. Call the admissions department to schedule your visit and find out what extended information sessions they offer. You should also check to see if they have a specific day set aside where all high school students are invited to explore the campus. If it's mid-week, you'll need to clear it with your high school.

TRIP TIPS

**Freshman,
Virginia Tech**

"I have a lot of unhappy friends because they had an 'image' of their college and it turned out completely different. Tours can provide a 'reality check.'"

Senior, Hope College

"We drove 3 hours just to 'look around' — never realizing that if we had called ahead, we would've been given a tour of the campus, the dorms, met a professor in my major . . . I walked away from a $24,000 scholarship because I was 'unimpressed' when I hadn't really given the school a chance."

Sophomore, William and Mary

"College is a whole lifestyle and you're not going to experience it on a tour. Plan on spending one or two nights with a student at (the) college."

**Sophomore
U. of Colorado**

"Lose your parents. Walk around campus by yourself. They're not coming to school with you."

**Sophomroe,
Penn State U.**
"I'd never even seen the campus! I just figured that millions of kids had come before me and made it . . . As long as you don't expect perfect . . ."

Freshmen, Converse College
"Visit the school. Visit the town. Visit the stores. Visit the people."

**Sophomore,
Georgetown U.**
"Trust your gut. If you don't feel right, it's not the school for you."

**Mom,
U. of Arizona**
"Give it the night-time test. If it's Tuesday night and there's a lot of partying and loud music coming out of the dorm rooms .. is that you? Are you going to be able to study?"

Junior, Miami U. Ohio
"DO NOT SET FOOT ON A CAMPUS IN AUGUST! My parents wanted to squeeze in a college visit before my senior year so our entire family flew out for a tour. The people there were really nice—both of them! The place was a ghost town! It weirded me out . . ."

65

best times for
campus visits

Mid-week. Mid-week visits allow you to get a feel for day-to-day life right down to eating in the cafeteria and sitting in on a class. You can meet with professors and/or admissions people. Be sure to call ahead.

Weekends. You'll get a good taste of the social scene... and seeing how many kids spend weekend nights studying will give you a clue as to the academic scene. If most students leave on weekends, it's a 'suitcase college.'

Summer. BUT only when classes are in session and the faculty you want to see will be there. Probably a little more laid back than usual ... check to see if the dorms are air-conditioned.

Holidays. Your holidays (Good Friday, Presidents Day, Spring Break) may not be theirs in which case a visit could be perfect. Forget Christmas. Everyone's gone in December the minute exams are over.

Exam Week. Check the college exam schedule. It may be all right for a day visit with admissions but certainly not an overnight.

* incomplete

you may want to ask...

Have questions ready for admissions officers and students. Ask the same ones on all visits so you can compare fairly. These can get you started:

For admissions officers:

What percentage of freshmen return for sophomore year?

What makes (college's) major/program special?

Is it easy to switch majors?

What kind of scholarships are offered? Availability? Eligibility?

Does the school provide tutors? Is there a fee or is it free? Is there a mentoring system for all students?

Is dorm living available for all four years? How much off-campus housing is available?

Do most students join fraternities and sororities? How do students who don't join socialize?

What do the tuition costs include? What other expenses can I expect?

Are campus jobs available? Are there businesses to provide part-time jobs and internships for students?

Is the campus safe? What types of crimes have there been? Is off-campus housing safe?

What are the important campus issues?

For students:

What's the best thing about this college? The worst?

Do the professors teach or TAs? How accessible are the professors?

How good are the student advisors?

Is this a 'suitcase' college? Do students stay or go home on weekends?

What about transportation? Where's the airport? Train station? Mass transportation? Do I need a car?

Where's the shopping district? Restaurants?

What's fun to do? Where are the movies? Concerts? Sporting events?

the admissions
interview...

Very few schools actually require a personal interview . . . however, **it can be to your advantage to request one.** It allows admissions to put a face with the name on the application and gives you a chance to provide more information than just what's on the application. When it's down to the wire as to who gets in and who doesn't, chances are you'll have an advantage over someone who didn't interview. Here are a few pointers to make your interview successful:

▷ **Read the college catalog** before your visit. Don't ask questions that are answered in the catalog.

▷ **Make a list of questions** you'd like to ask and also make a list of things you'd like them to know about you.

▷ **Keep your parents out** of the interview.

▷ **Send a thank you *note*** . . . not an email.

virtual touring

Almost every college web site has a virtual campus tour. But remember, colleges post what they want you to see. Use VTs before your college visit to help form a list of questions and for places you'd like to see. Visit the college web site or try:

www.campustours.com

www.collegeview.com

. . . look for links

Look for links to students' web pages when you're visiting a college web site. They provide more 'up close and personal' info as well as e-mail addresses of students so that you can get the 'inside line' directly from the students themselves.

campus visits

Before:

☐ **Call** the admissions department one month before your visit. Make appointments with the admissions officer, teachers or anyone else you need to see.

☐ **Ask** to sit in on a class in your major and, if possible, sleep overnight in a dorm.

☐ **Request** a course catalog and campus map. Review them before you go.

☐ **Do** a virtual tour before going, making notes of what you'd like to see.

☐ **Make** a list of questions to ask at all colleges (page 67).

During:

☐ **Find** the hangout. Eat in the cafeteria. Eavesdrop on conversations and find out what students are talking about. Notice student behavior, dress, prominent groups. Do you fit in?

☐ **Notice** the campus layout (i.e. the location of dorms to the classrooms, parking, etc.).

☐ **Check** out the condition of the dorms, bathrooms, showers, and common rooms. Find out what's included and what you will need to supply.

☐ **Read** the student paper, local paper, and bulletin boards for activities, clubs, opportunities, and campus and local issues.

☐ **Check** out the classrooms and labs (i.e. music rooms, studios, theater, science labs). Are the facilities up-to-date and will they accomodate what you want to study?

☐ **Check** out computer availability. PCs or Macs? What's the student to computer ratio?

☐ **Visit** the library. Is it large enough for study groups? Quiet enough for private studying? Comfortable? Enough seating?

☐ **Tour** the physical education facilities. What kind of equipment is available? When is it available to you?

☐ **Listen** to your gut instinct. Do you feel comfortable? Safe? Is this the school for you?

After:

☐ **Make** notes. Set up categories so you can compare colleges. Write down your general feelings: Were you comfortable? Inspired? Intimidated? Out-of-place?

☐ **Write**—don't e-mail—thank you notes to any representative you've met: admissions officer, financial aid officer, and professors.

11

junior year
on your mark, get set . . .

The time is now to make sure you're on the right track for the colleges you want to apply to. Intensify your scholarship search, study for SATs/ACTs, attend college fairs, do in-depth college visits, find out about financial aid... and most important of all FOCUS ON YOUR GRADES! College admission folks rely heavily on your junior year GPA! They want to see grades rising—not falling. Beyond that, every extra thing you can do this year is going to make your life a lot easier as a senior.

66 Whenever I could, I avoided teachers who were tough graders—especially if they required a lot of papers.
It was good for my GPA but the downside is I had a really hard time my first year of college . . . especially in my freshman writing course. **99**

Sophomore, Spelman College

junior year

Through The Year . . .

☐ **Concentrate** on your GPA. Keep your grades high and your courses as challenging as possible.

☐ **Get** information packets from the colleges you're considering. Request them from college web sties or call the admissions department.

☐ **Intensify** your scholarship search. Keep track of deadlines and requirements.

☐ **Attend** career days, college fairs (page 77) and financial aid workshops.

☐ **Start** your in-depth college visits this year (page 63).

Fall:

☐ **Meet** with your counselor. Be sure your classes are on the right track for the colleges you're considering and that you're meeting graduation requirements.

☐ **Register** for and take the PSAT. *This year it counts for the National Merit Scholarship.*

☐ **Talk** to your coach if you want to play for a college team or apply for an athletic scholarship (page 82).

☐ **Schedule** dates to take the SAT and ACT tests. Arrange to take both tests at least once during your junior year (page 83).

☐ **Investigate** financial aid programs now before the financial 'base' year begins (page 91).

☐ **Contact** the US military academies NOW if you want to apply. Find out about the individual schools and their summer programs at:

www.defenselink.mil/faq/pis/20.html

☐ **Research** summer workshops and college courses for high school students.

Winter:

☐ **Review** your PSAT results with your counselor. Pump up any weak subjects.

☐ **Register** for the SAT, ACT and SAT II tests if the colleges you're considering require them (page 85). If you're applying Early Decision (page 123), and want to take them a second time, be sure to take the SAT and ACT again in June.

☐ **Decide** what camps, programs, volunteer work and classes you want to attend or take in summer.

Spring:

☐ **Compile** writing samples, put together portfolios, and work on audition tapes if the colleges or scholarships you're applying to require them.

☐ **Consider** taking a summer class. You can start earning college credit by taking 'dual credit courses' or classes at a community college (page 115).

☐ **Take** AP exams for the AP classes you've completed (page 78).

☐ **See** your counselor for an NCAA clearinghouse form if you want to play sports in college (page 82).

☐ **Look** for a summer job. Try to get one related to a major you're considering.

Summer:

☐ **Request** applications for scholarships.

☐ **Start** work on your essays for college applications and scholarships (page 105).

☐ **Zero** in on what teachers you want to ask for recommendations (page 122).

☐ **Work** on your resume (page 101).

☐ **Start** your application process if you're applying Early Decision or Early Action (page 123).

let's play . . .

Ask the right questions and you may win admission to the college of your choice!

Am I on the right track to complete my graduation requirements? Will I have enough math, science, and language classes for college?

Can I get a pass/fail grade option for electives so it doesn`t affect my GPA?

What scholarships do you know about? What scholarships have been awarded to students? Does the school have a scholarship search program?

Are there any finacial aid workshops or seminars for my parents?

Should I take advanced placement classes, dual credit courses (page 115), correspondence, on-line courses, or any summer classes?

What are dates for the SAT and ACT this year? Does the school offer prep classes or materials?

Will the school be hosting a college fair or college night? Will a large college fair be held locally? Do local or state colleges hold weekend information worshops?

Are there any contests, panels, or any other opportunities to represent my school?

(If you`re interested in the military) How can the military help me? Whom should I contact for more information?

> 66 I hadn't even heard of this college,
> let alone it's aviation program.
> I talked with their rep at College Night . . .
> and here I am. 99

Freshman, Northwestern College

come to the *college* fair!

College fairs give you a chance to talk with representatives from colleges you're considering and expose you to schools you never knew existed.

▶ Your high school may offer one or there may be one offered at another school in your district. Check with your guidance office.

▶ Watch the newspapers or check with other school districts in your state. Call to see if you're allowed to attend.

▶ To find out if the college you`re interested in will be at any fair, go to the college`s web site or call the admissions office.

super-sized! the NACAC fairs

The National Association for College Admissions Counseling hosts huge nationwide fairs with hundreds of colleges - big and small, public and private - in attendance. You may have to drive to another city, even another state, but attending is well worth it. For dates and locations go to:

www.nacac.com

why knock yourself out?
the AP dilemma

 AP coursework prepares students better for the rigors of a college classroom.

 Selective schools EXPECT that you will have taken them.

 GPA rules! That's particularly true for less selective schools as well as for many scholarships. AP's aren't a factor... an 'A' is an 'A'.

 AP courses are smaller, cheaper, and most students say 'a whole lot easier' than the equivalent college course. Load up.

 You'll end up taking upper level classes as a college freshman—before you've gotten used to the pace of college coursework.

 Does admissions look more favorably at a 'B' in an AP class than an 'A' in a regular class? Ask 50 admissions officers and get 50 different answers! Your best bet... take the AP class and work your tail off to get an 'A'.

66 AP's are serious business...they're for serious students . . . I've had students take them just to be in a class with a friend or just to be able to say they were taking it—the results were disastrous. 99

High School Counselor

For more info: www.collegeboard.com

The International Baccalaureate (IB) Program... offers a choice of the Diploma Program (two years—junior and senior—of intense study) or opt for IB certification in specific subject areas. Relatively few American high schools offer IBs but their popularity is increasing. Watch out: many students say IBs are more difficult than college classes. But they all say IBs prepare you for college-level work. For more information and the schools that offer the IB Program, go to:

www.ibo.org

66 It's worth taking as many APs as you feel you can do well in. In college I was able to fill my schedule with interesting electives instead of boring basics. 99

Junior, Rice U.

66 I took two AP English classes and THEN found out the college only allowed credit for one... Check out which college accepts which AP credits before you take them because they're a lot of work! 99

Freshman, U. of Chicago

66 Don't overdo it... I took five AP classes and got so burned out I didn't even take the tests. 99

Freshman, U. of Nevada

money well spent . . .

"...you pay $78 to take an AP exam... but if you receive a qualifying grade on that exam you'll earn college credits, **which can be worth anywhere from $300 at a state university to $3,000 at a private school.**"

Sue Collins in *Newsweek's How to Get Into College*

see the
world...

There are organizations that can help with information, opportunities, arrangements, student IDs, and discount fares. Whether you want to take time off before you start college to study abroad during high school or college, or be involved in a volunteer or work exchange program these sites can help. Not the globetrotting sort? Do it in North America. Some of the opportunities:

great stuff!

IIEPassport.org

THE search engine for high school and college students searches by language, country, or study. This site has quick notification on programs that fit you and ones that may be of interest, an on-line student guide for FAQs and more.

americorps.org

Stay on home turf. Volunteer as a mentor, build houses, clean parks and streams, or respond to disasters in a 10 month full-time residential program for 17 years and older. Get a great experience AND about $4700 to pay for college (and perhaps a living allowance).

planetedu.com

Volunteer in Russia, China, Peru... explore a biosphererereserve or go on a culinary tour. Do a high school semester or spend summer living with a host family and study overseas. Language schools and study abroad programs are available for HS and college students.

www.vfp.org (Volunteers For Peace)

For $200 (plus airfare) for a 2 - 3 week program, international volunteers perform community service in overseas workcamps. Students from at least 4 countries make up each group. Cultural and social sharing and discussion are encouraged. Work camps for ages under 18 are limited to France and Germany.

youthinternational.org

It's pricey ($7500/semester) but includes nearly everything: flights, rooms, food and great activities. Two destinations—Asia and South America—are offered to students 18 and older.

ISTC.org

Get your International Student Identity Card and save on travel, rooms, museums, events and entertainment. Specializing in student travel, the network of 500 organizations covers 100 countries. Also the site offers overseas work exchange programs.

You can study abroad while in college, too. The 'study abroad' office at your college will be able to find a program that suits your major.

studyabroad.com

HS'ers can spend summer on European college campuses (scholarships available!). Or find out what's available before and during college.

counciltravel.com

CT excels in travel possibilities for students and will even help you design your own around-the-world trip. Apply for a student discount card (ISIC), or book student fares for air or rail. Language courses, work/internships, and study abroad programs are also offered.

www.unv.org

The United Nations volunteer program offers opportunities overseas, on home soil or on-line. Also links to organizations specializing in short-term and long-terms volunteer service, medical service, wildlife conservation, humanitarian efforts, disaster relief, and more.

cityyear.org

The youth service corps asks for volunteers, ages 17 and older for a full year of community service, leadership development and civic engagement. Programs are in major US cities.

the
jock clock

If you want to play a sport in college, your junior year is the time to start asking questions. *Start by talking to your high school coach during the fall. Then see your counselor for any NCAA forms you may need.* The NCAA (National Collegiate Athletic Association) has very strict guidelines concerning recruiting and student to coach/college contact. Breaking those rules could disqualify you from playing sports. Check out the NCAA website for more information and guidelines:

www.ncaa.org/cbsa/

" It was a win-win.
I loved playing ball and
—scholarship or not—
there were colleges
interested in me that
wouldn't have been otherwise . . . "

Graduate, U. of Michigan

tests: sat & act

don't panic

Even if you're the world's worst test-taker there's hope for you. Along with being able to take the SAT and ACT numerous times to improve your score, you can take practice tests to ease your anxiety. There's help everywhere. An industry has been built around helping you get a better test score. And in case your test score doesn't reflect your stellar GPA, relax. Admission departments know that some students don't test well and take that into consideration. In fact, a few colleges don't even consider the tests at all . . .

SAT & ACT
the difference is

SAT → is a 3 hour test that measures your abilities.

ACT → is a 3 hour test that measures your knowledge.

SAT → tests vocabulary, geometry and algebra. Doesn't test trigonometry.

ACT → tests English, math, reading and science. Does test trigonometry.

SAT → has some multiple choice.

ACT → is all multiple choice.

SAT → penalizes you for guessing.

ACT → doesn't penalize your for guessing.

SAT → is given 7 times a year.

ACT → is given 5 times a year.

*(beginning in March, 2005,
the SAT will include a written essay)*

which one do I take?

Most schools will take either the SAT or the ACT but check with the colleges you're considering to be sure. If you have the option of taking either test, take both. Some students do better on one test than the other.

should you retest?

Studies show that you can increase your score by about 20%—but not without a lot of studying. Check your colleges to find their average SAT/ACT score. Then check your scholarship leads for qualifying scores. Are your scores high enough? Then, you're done. If not, retest. But be real. **Don't overstudy for these tests at the expense of your GPA.**

get 'the real thing'

'Retired' tests—actual tests that were used in past years—are the only way to KNOW the test. Duplicate the setting as much as you can. Time the test and take the whole test in one sitting. Retired tests are available at: ***ACT: The ACT Assessment Sample Test Booklet*** available at **www.act.org** store for $5. ***SAT: 10 Real SATs*** available from College Board at bookstores and through the **www.collegeboard.com** store.

(SAT)
www.collegeboard.com

(ACT)
www.act.org

Go to the test web sites and get this year's test dates, registration dates, and locations. (The web sites also offer practice tests, on-line registration and the option of getting your scores on line). Then set up a test calendar for yourself:

 **The first test** is in September/October of your junior year.

The last time you'll be able to test and still get the results to your college on time is November/December of your senior year— if you overnight your scores to your school.

Allow 4 to 6 weeks to get your scores and time for studying before retesting.

Allow time for one test in your senior year just in case you need it.

Applying Early Decision? Check with the college for the last safe test date.

the
SAT II
Subject Achievement Tests for English History, Math, Science, and Language

Before you start sweating the SAT IIs, know this: only 60 schools out of 4,000 plus require them. **Some students choose to take them to impress the admissions office or to get an exemption from college freshman classes.** Check your colleges' requirements and with your counselor to see if you could benefit from taking the SATIIs. College Board's web site has a list of available tests and the dates they're administered. **The best tip on taking an SAT II: take it right after you've completed the course.**

a little help, puleeze

There's test prep help for everyone. Find out if your school is offering a prep class, look for summer test prep camps, and check out the bookstores and libraries for books and software programs. Test prep web sites sell their services but all of them offer—for free—tips, on-line classrooms, practice tests and strategies. Try 'em all:

www.collegeboard.com	www.act.org
www.onlinetestprep.com	www.kaptest.com
www.act-sat-prep.com	www.4tests.com
www.petersons.com	www.review.com
www.powerprep.com	www.number2.com

. . . hate tests?

You still have to take them, but the nearly 400 schools—private and public, large and small—listed at Fair Test's web site will use you SAT or ACT score **for placement only** or other minimal requirements. For a complete list of schools and the pros and cons of taking the SAT and ACT, go to: **www.fairtest.org/univ/optional.htm**

test day tips

"Take a practice test—on paper. The real test is on paper. It's the only way to get a real 'feel' for the test."
Freshman, Ohio State U.

Test 'stand-by' if you missed registration. Call the testing organization to see if you can take the place of a 'no-show'.

"Read the instructions on the sample tests until you've got 'em down 'cold'. You can pick up a couple of minutes during the real test."
Sophomore, U. of Michigan

Know where you made your mistakes! **Get a copy of your SAT test from College Board** ($12). It'll help you focus your studying forthe retest.

Want your school to see only your best score and not the dogs? **The ACT gives you the option of reporting only your best score.** Forfeit the free score reporting at the time of the test. Then notify ACT which score to send. It'll cost $7 per college.

"I took an energy bar with me and ate it between sections . . .at least it kept my stomach from growling."
Freshman, U. of Michigan

"I knew where the school was (test location) but I didn't know the street was torn up. I wasn't late but I didn't have time to relax, either. Do a 'test drive' before test day."
Sophomore, U. of Wisconsin

Make sure your **name appears the same way on all your tests and college applications.** The test companies and colleges will have a harder time matching tests to applications if you don't.

87

what's it take?*

As you can see by this sampling of SAT and ACT scores from schools around the US, 'selectivity' is not based solely on test scores. (ACT: 2 digits, SAT: 3-4 digits)

Perfect scores: SAT—1600, ACT—36

most selective

Harvard 1380-1570
MIT 1410-1560
Notre Dame 1260-1450
Duke 29-33
University of Michigan 26-30
Oberlin 1240-1430
US Airforce Academy 1190-1360

more selective

Purdue 1020-1250
George Washington University 1150-1330
Auburn University 21-26
Antioch College 22-28
University of Texas 1090-1320
Tulane University 1240-1410

selective

University of Arizona 990-1230
Concordia University 23
Illinois State University 20-25
University of Colorado 1070-1260
Howard University 850-1330

less selective

Albany State University 820-980
Bethany College 850-1120
Fisk University 16-21
Morgan State University 830-1010
Marian College 860-1060

least selective

Alabama State University 14-19
University of Bridgeport 740-1060
Northeastern Illinois 14-19
Southern Vermont College 820-1070

* US News & World Report, 2001

'the tests'

- ☐ **SAT, ACT or both?** Check with your colleges to see what they require and if you need to take any SAT II tests.

- ☐ **Lay out** your own calendar for when you'll take the test(s). Get this year's test dates from the testing organizations' web sites or check with your counselor.

- ☐ **Register** at least six weeks prior to the test date. If you want to be assured that you will test at your first choice location, register much earlier—especially if your school is a test site. Test packets may be picked up in the guidance office or you may register directly with the testing organization at their web sites.

- ☐ **Test** 'stand-by' if you missed the registration deadline. There's a cost involved. Contact the test organization or ask your counselor.

- ☐ **Ask** your counselor for a fee waiver if you can't afford the test. Also ask for disability accomodations if you need them.

- ☐ **Prep** for the test. Take the practice tests at the testing web sites. Be sure to include at least one 'retired' test in your preparation (page 85).

- ☐ **Find** out if prep classes or individual tutoring will be available at or through your school.

☐ **Check** out the library and bookstores for prep materials and software programs that suit your needs.

☐ **Read** and keep the test admission information packet you receive. File the information and phone numbers for future use.

The day of testing:

☐ **Take** with you:
- Your high school code
- The code numbers of colleges to where you want your test scores sent
- Admission ticket
- Picture ID or driver license
- Approved calculator
- Extra pencils
- Facial tissue
- Water and a snack (only allowed at break)
- Wear a watch to monitor your time

☐ **Repeat** testing if you need or think you are capable of getting a better score — but do something to increase your chances of improving first.

. . . score more!

Vocabulary is a hard thing to improve in a short amount of time. Get a jump on it at: **freevocabulary.com**, a site that lists 5,000 collegiate works and their definitions. There's a downloadable 36 page PDF version or pop for the audio tape for about $30.

aid
money 101

get it right—now!

It's important to get familiar with the financial aid process now not only because it's so darn complicated but because **the fiscal year on which your financial aid package is based begins in your JUNIOR year of high school.** You won't apply for aid until the fall and winter of your senior year, but if your family needs to plan its finances, **they need to do it before the base year begins. And don't ignore FAFSA guidelines because you think your family is ineligible for financial aid.** You'll lose out on the opportunity to at least take advantage of government loan programs. **The truth is. . . virtually every college student in the U.S. qualifies for some type of financial aid.**

the language of
financial aid

FAFSA: Free Application for Federal Student Aid. You must fill this form out even if you do not expect to receive aid from a college. **You can't get a federally-backed student loan without this form.**

CSS/Profile: College Scholarship Service Profile, a non-government FAFSA. Not all colleges require this form. Check with the schools you want to apply to for the proper forms (some colleges even require their own financial application).

EFC: Expected Family Contribution. The amount your family is expected to pay based on their specific circumstances and finances.

SAR: Student Aid Report. You will be sent this form after completing the FAFSA. Colleges use this form to determine your aid package.

Need-based: College grants and scholarships that are issued based on your financial need.

Merit-based: College grants and scholarships that are issued based on your academic, athletic or artistic talent. Ethnicity is also sometimes considered.

Grants: Money from the government or college that **does not** have to be repaid.

Loan: Money from the government or private lender that **does** have to be repaid.

Scholarships: Do not have to be repaid. Can be **institutional** (from the college) or **private** (outside source).

Work study: Need-based program of subsidized jobs through the college. Students usually work up to 20 hours per week.

Subsidized: Interest on a loan **does not** accrue while student is in school

Non-subsidized: Interest on the loan **does** accrue while student is in school.

PELL Grants: Federal money for low-income students that **does not** have to be repaid.

Perkins Loan: A federally-backed need-based loan direct from a participating college. Interest does not accrue while student is in school.

Stafford Loan: Government sponsored loans to students. Subsidized Stafford Loans are need-based; non-subsidized are not. Either can be obtained from banks, savings and loans, or other lenders.

PLUS Loans: Government sponsored loans to parents come at a higher interest rate than Stafford loans.

State grants: Money from a state that is given to resident students who are attending in-state schools. Programs differ from state to state.

just the facts,
ma'am

Financial aid packages vary from college to college and depend on family circumstances, a student's abilities and talents, and how each Financial Aid Officer (FAO) interprets a student's needs. **One thing is certain: the more you understand financial aid, the more likely you are to receive it.**

Some basics that cover *EVERYONE*:

▷ **Almost every family qualifies** for some type of aid even if it's only a federally backed loan at lower interest rate.

▷ **The amount your family is expected to pay (EFC)** stays roughly the same at expensive schools as at cheaper schools. It's the aid package that is adjustable.

▷ **Financial forms do not reflect** family circumstances that may limit your ability to pay (i.e. medical expenses). You can talk to the Financial Aid Officer (FAO) directly and have your EFC adjusted.

▷ **Don't put family assets in a** student's name. Student's money is always assessed at a higher rate.

▷ **You can negotiate** financial aid pack-ages from colleges (page 138).

▷ **You'll pay more** at out-of-state public schools. Base tuition is usually doubled at least.

▷ **Aid packages offered** to the student for the freshman year may change for the next three years.

A student's income

---

is assessed at a

---

higher rate than parents'.

After exemptions, parents are expected

---

to contribute about 5% of their income.

Students are assessed at 35%.

---

money moves

It's your income that takes center stage when your eligibility for financial aid is being considered. Some families elect to 'lower' their income by controlling when one-time or unusual income (such as a bonus or money from a real estate transaction) is made. Because college financial aid packages use a base calendar year that begins January 1 of your junior year and ends December 31 of your senior year you need to understand the ins and outs of financial aid or consult your financial advisor now. Any 'money moves' need to be done before or after that base period.

In order to get the maximum...

In order to get the maximum money available

---

to you, take out a Perkins or Stafford Loan

---

before applying for a PLUS Loan.

everything you ever needed to know about financial aid . . .

the sites

Use these web sites to find out about the financial aid process, scholarships, grants, loans, work study programs, use a financial calculator, and download forms and instructions. Visit as many as you can—they're loaded with tips, strategies and advice.

www.finaid.org
www.fastweb.com
www.salliemae.com
www.ed.gov/index.jsp
www.collegeboard.com
www.srnexpress.com
www.eduprep.com
www.wiredscholar.com
www.xap.com
www.collegeispossible.org
www.petersons.com
www.collegeview.com

state aid

All states provide need and merit based aid. The good news is they're usually more generous than the federal government. Even if the feds turn you down, your state may do something for you. But state aid is usually given to residents who plan to attend school in-state and residency requirements are strict. If you're thinking about attending another state's public university, **check with your state to see if it has a reciprocal agreement with other states.** That would allow you to transfer your aid. For links to your state's aid office, go to:

www.students.gov

. . . and where to find it

hard copy

Books that address specific financial aid situations line the shelves at bookstores and libraries. For a good general overview of the financial aid process with plenty of advice, tips, strategies, guidelines, worksheets, forms and directories, try:

College Financial Aid for Dummies
(Dr. Herm Davis & Joyce Lain Kennedy)

Paying for College Without Going Broke
(Kalman A. Chany, Princeton Review)

You Can Afford College
(Alice Murphey, Kaplan)

The Complete Idiot's Guide to Financial Aid for College
(David Rye)

College Cost & Financial Aid Handbook
(College Board)

'the' magazine

Want to know what any college costs? Tuition? Room and board? How many students receive financial aid? How much financial aid do they receive? Pick up a copy of *US News & World Report: America's Best Colleges.* Here's a sample of what you'll get:

PRINCETON:

Expenses:2002-2003: $27,230; room/board: $7,842
Financial Aid: (609) 258-3330. 50% of undergrads applied for financial aid. 43% of undergrads determined to have financial need; average aid package $23,810. Those receiving need-based aid have 100% of need met; 100% of undergrads' need is fully met; 43% of undergrads receive need-based grants, average grant $21,840.

Important to know!

the financial campus visit
dicker & deal

The financial aid package should be part of the college selection so do a financial campus visit—even if it's only by phone. It's only fair that the FAO answer questions such as:

- **Will my financial need affect** my admission chances?

- **How will applying 'Early Decision'** affect my financial aid package?

- **Does the college use** its own financial form? What are the college's deadlines?

- **How much do the total costs rise** each year?

- **What costs are not included** in the aid package? Room and board? Books?

- **Is there an academic requirement** for aid renewal? Any other conditions?

- **How will my aid package differ** from year to year? Will it decrease?

- **What is the average loan debt** for a student at the time of graduation?

- **Does the college assign work-study** jobs? What kind of jobs are available? How many hours per week?

- **Does the college include PLUS Loans** in the financial aid package (page 138)?

- **If the financial aid package is insufficient,** under what conditions will the FAO reconsider?

money 101

Junior Fall:

☐ **Get** your parents involved in the financial aid process now. Check out the web sites and books for information that fits your circumstances.

☐ **Make** any financial decisions before the 'base' calendar year begins on January 1.

☐ **Take** the PSAT to qualify for the National Merit Scholarship.

☐ **Write** to your college choices and request catalogs and financial aid information.

☐ **Get** a copy of FAFSA and CSS/Profile from your counselor, the library, or on-line and study the forms for what you'll need next year. Find out what additional financial forms a specific college might request.

☐ **Attend** financial aid programs or seminars offered by your high school.

Junior Winter:

☐ **Find** out what kind of financial aid is offered by your state (page 96).

☐ **Get** the US Government's publications *Student Guide, Funding Your Education*, and *Looking for Student Aid*, downloadable at **www.ed.gov/pubs/parents/finaid.html** or call **1-800-4FED-AID**.

Junior Spring

☐ **Start** scouting banks, savings and loans, and other lenders for their student loan programs.

☐ **Open** an account with a bank if it's necessary to secure a student loan at that institution.

☐ **Intensify** your scholarship search (page 19).

☐ **Write** to scholarship organizations and request applications. Keep track of deadlines and requirements.

☐ **Ask** teachers/counselors to write any recommendations you'll need senior year. They'll have more time in the summer—in the fall they're overwhelmed with requests.

Junior Summer:

☐ **Make** a list of the financial records you'll need to complete your financial forms.

☐ **Do** a financial aid campus visit (on-site or by telephone) during the summer when FAOs aren't busy (page 98).

☐ **Contact** the colleges' athletic departments for athletic scholarships.

how

to build your 'resume'

bragging rights

There's a bonus to putting a resume together now. If you have any weak spots, you'll be able to see where they are while there's still time to do something about them. A resume is a place to show off your hard work. **It can speak volumes for you, especially when you're not there to do it yourself.** Use your resume to apply for jobs and internships, attach one to scholarship applications, and give one to those whom you've asked to write a letter of recommendation. Last but not least —save some for those college applications!

putting
'you' on paper

Create a resume that highlights your strengths and interests. Many scholarships and programs have their own form or format but if you start out with a basic layout you can use it to transfer the information quickly. For formats and guides try:

www.damngood.com/yana/map.html

This site is for the fill-in-the-blank workbook: *The Resume Workbook for High School Students* by Yana Parker. You can view sample resumes on the net. Buy the book (or get it from the libary) and use one of the easy fill-in-the-blank formats.

www.teenadvice.about.com/cs/writingaresume

Along with sample resumes, sample cover letters are included. This site has great tips and information.

Creating Your High School Resume by Kathryn Kraemer Troutman can help you target your resume for specific purposes: college applications, scholarships, internships or jobs. Cover letter samples and how-tos are included also.

66 Don't cheat yourself by leaving out accomplishments that are not formalized . . . If you've been a caregiver to a sick parent or you've invented a computer game — include it on your resume. 99

Counselor, Salem High School

to do's
resumes

Include:

☐ **Personal information**
- Name
- Address
- Phone number
- E-mail address

☐ **Scholastic information**
- Name of high school
- Class rank, GPA
- SAT, ACT and SATII scores

☐ **Academic achievements**
- Honor roll
- Advanced placement classes
- College credit classes
- Internet classes
- Awards, nominations, recognitions, citations or special projects in subject areas
- Tutoring or mentoring roles

☐ **Computer Skills**
- Programs you know
- Skills (web site design, programming)

☐ **Workshops**, camps, programs, seminars, projects, special classes, and competitions

☐ **Work** experience, internships

☐ **Club involvement**
- School
- Community
- Church

☐ **Special interests** hobbies, pursuits

☐ **Volunteer work** on-going and one time events

☐ **Athletic** participation and achievements

☐ **Leadership roles**
- Holding office in class, sports, clubs
- Taking initiative or responsibility for projects
- Leadership camp participation

❝ There's only an itty-bitty space to 'tell something significant about yourself' on most college applications. Resumes are a great way to 'sneak' in a little more. It's good marketing. **❞**

High School Counselor

the essay

seal the deal

While one essay won't guarantee your getting into a college, a good one helps—and a bad one can 'tank' your application. And you won't be writing just one essay. You'll need at least one for each college application, not to mention scholarships. Save a part of the summer before your senior year to brainstorm ideas and work on rough drafts so you have plenty of time for rewrites and polishing. Don't forget the basic ingredient of a good essay: YOU! Essays are your chance to add dimension to those numbers and checked boxes on your application. Bring a little life to that package!

essay
do's · · · · · · · · · · · ·

DO answer the question.
Questions are often open-ended to allow you room
for expression. But make sure your essay fits.

DO get personal.
This essay's about you! Be passionate.
If it sounds like 300 other people
could have written it, you're missing something.

DO write a good lead.
Hook 'em with the first sentence
and they'll want to read the rest.

DO read
other essays to see what works.

DO check your essay
to see how you come across. Likeable?
Friendly? Interesting?

DO give your essay a rest.
Write it and then put it down for a
couple of days or weeks if you can.
Fresh eyes can tell you what's missing.

DO ask for help —
from your English teacher or an editing service.

DO edit and rewrite.
Even Hemmingway did.

. . . . **and don'ts**

DON'T try to be funny. . .
unless you really are and can carry it off like a pro.

DON'T suck up!
They know you want to go to their college.
Why else would you be doing all of this?

DON'T go over the word count.
Officials have to read thousands of essays. Too long
and you may be disqualified on a technicality.

DON'T use big words when little ones will do.
If you use them incorrectly, it'll count against you.
Plus you run the risk of looking arrogant.

DON'T let your parents
write your essay. You don't want to sound
like you're 45 years old.

DON'T plagerize or buy an essay.
This is about YOU. Besides there are
plagerizing programs that officials use and
they'll spot you in a minute.

DON'T use your friends or
relatives to critique your essay. They're too biased.
Use an English teacher or an editing service.

DON'T be negative!
Don't whine, complain or ask for sympathy.
Don't ever try to explain
a bad GPA or ACT/SAT score.

> ❝ . . . one student lost a $5,000 scholarship because he submitted an essay that was written for a different college.
> He was admitted but lost a great scholarship because he was lazy and took a shortcut. ❞

Admissions Counselor, U. of Washington

insightful sites

For detailed how-to information, advice, tips, and samples, you can't beat essay internet sites. Some of the ones listed offer editing services, too. Check out the freebies even if you don't opt for the paid help:

www.essayedge.com

www.world.std.com/~edit/tips4.htm

www.acm.edu/admiss

www.personalessay.com

www.essaywizard.net

www.teenink.com/College/Essays.html

www.accepted.com

www.campusnut.com/collapps.cfm

www.collegeboard.com

www.review.com

. . . along with general essay help,
there are books that specifically target essays for **Ivy League** schools or Top 50 schools. For general assistance, try: ***On Writing the College Application Essay*** by Harry Bauld. ***How to Write a Winning College Application Essay*** by Michael James Mason. ***The College Application Essay*** by Sarah Myers McGinty.

the essay

- ☐ **Review** last year's essay topics on-line at your colleges' web sites.

- ☐ **Find** out if your scholarship applications require essays.

- ☐ **Check** out the bookstores and libraries for books on writing college essays.

- ☐ **Brainstorm** a list of topics that you could use.

- ☐ **Narrow** down your topic selection by writing brief outlines and eliminate weak ideas.

- ☐ **Write** a draft of your essay(s). Don't read it for a few days, then . . .

- ☐ **Edit** and rewrite your essay(s). Make sure it answers the question asked.

- ☐ **Tailor**, blend in, or change your essay in some way to be more appropriate and fit the question asked if you're submitting it to more than one college.

- ☐ **Proofread**—don't spell check—your essay. Computer spellcheckers can't tell the difference between 'know' and 'no'.

- ☐ **Ask** two objective people (i.e. English teacher/ counselor) to review your essay.

- ☐ **Make** sure your final copy is neat and clean.

66 The first 3 years
of high school is what
gets you INTO college . . .
your senior year
is what KEEPS you there. 99

Admissions Officer, U. of Michigan

12

senior year
. . . .GO!

If you've had your act together along the way, senior year is the 'payoff'— good times, good friends, getting into the college of your choice, and looking ahead to the future. While you may be tempted to 'ease up' on academics—don't. Senior year is your launch pad. . .the more challenging your classes, the easier your adjustment in a college classroom. This is not the end of your journey, it's the beginning and you'll want to make sure that you're well prepared for what lies ahead.

to do's
senior year

Fall:

☐ **Create** a master calendar of deadlines. Include college applications, test registrations and test dates, scholarship applications, housing, and financial deadlines.

☐ **Look** for scholarships one last time. Request any applications you don't already have.

☐ **Last chance** to take the SAT or ACT. Register early.

☐ **Request** college applications, financial aid and housing applications.

☐ **Make** sure your high school transcripts and records are correct and up-to-date.

☐ **Review** your college plans and financial aid preparations (page 135) with your counselor.

☐ **Attend** college fairs and financial aid workshops.

☐ **Make** the last of your college visits. If you haven't had an interview with the admissions office, request one.

☐ **Ask** for letters of recommendation from teachers, employers, and coaches (page 122).

☐ **Finish** essays for college applications and scholarships (page 105).

☐ **Update** your resume.

☐ **Apply** 'Early Decision' or 'Early Action' if you so choose (page 123).

☐ **Send** in applications to your other college choices.

Winter:

☐ **Gather** tax information for the financial aid applications.

☐ **Fill** out financial aid forms (page 135). Apply for scholarships.

☐ **Have** your mid-year grades sent to colleges. Follow up to make sure they were sent.

Spring:

☐ **Decide** on a college and notify the admissions office by May 1st of your acceptance. Notify other colleges who have accepted you that you will not be attending.

☐ **Create** a budget to determine your needs (page 151).

☐ **Determine** if you need a student loan. File your application.

☐ **See** your doctor for a physical and any necessary vaccinations (page 149).

☐ **Complete** your housing and meal application(s).

☐ **Take** Advanced Placement Exams.

☐ **Have** your final transcript sent to your college.

Summer:

☐ **Notify** your college of any scholarships you received.

☐ **Apply** for a summer job. If your financial aid package includes work study, you may be responsible for finding a job at college.

☐ **Start** your reading assignments for freshman year.

☐ **Take** a deep breath. Pack for college.

getting a
head start...

Earn college credit NOW! Want to get basic college classes out of the way? Save tuition? Groove into college-level work?

▷ **Dual Credit classes** let you earn high school and college credit. These classes are offered on a college or community college campus, sometimes at a high school, and even on the internet at college web sites.

▷ **Community College classes** are a great way to get core college classes out of the way since credits are usually transferable. Consider taking one or two classes during your senior year and/or one during the summer before college.

▷ **Distance learning** is done by taking college courses online (page 130).

beware. . .

Some colleges may refuse to accept some or all credits or will want you to take an AP exam to prove you've learned the material. Talk with admissions at the colleges you're considering to see what are the best classes to take before investing time, effort and money.

66 Kids apply to schools
they don't even want to go to
just to say they 'got in.'
It's like 'get a grip . . .' 99

Freshman, Michigan State U.

the
art of applying

deadlines, details, decisions

Don't trip up on a technicality.
Every college has its own deadline and usually
there's more than one. In-state students may have
different deadlines than out-of-state students.
Then there are separate deadlines for housing
and financial aid. Each college has its own
application forms. Even colleges that use a
'common application' will have an additional
form for you to complete. Miss a deadline or
fill out an application incorrectly and—no
matter how perfect you are for that school—you
may disqualify yourself from being accepted.
Pay attention to deadlines and details so you can
deal with the most important 'D': deciding which
college you'll attend.

applications...
where and how many?

Application fees range from $25 to $60.
You'll want to apply to more than one, but applying to more than six colleges may be wasting money that could be used for books. Apply to academically appropriate schools with various levels of selectivity:

▶ **'Reach'** schools are the most selective schools on your list; probably your first and second choices. Your chances of getting in are about 20%.

▶ Schools whose numbers (SAT/ACT scores, GPA and class rank) match your numbers should be your second group. **Your chances of getting in are about 50/50.**

▶ Include at least one **'safety'** school—a college that fits your needs. Because of your credentials and their selectivity, **you'd be a shoe-in.**

66 Look at what the WHOLE school
has to offer—not just what
you want to major in.
You may want to
change your major.
And remember,
you'll be spending
at least 4 years of your life there. 99

Freshman, Texas Christian U.

admissions...
rolling and deadline

Apply to six colleges and it's likely you'll find six different application policies. Read applications carefully and follow directions to the letter. **Omitted or incorrect information will cause your application to be returned.** Pay attention to the type of admissions each school uses:

▷ **Deadline admissions:** Applications are sent in by a deadline and only then does the school begin it's admission process.

▷ **Rolling admissions:** Applications are accepted or rejected as they arrive. Most large state schools use this process. The schools get choosier as they get closer to the deadline date. **Applying early is vital.**

▷ **Special filing dates:** Out-of-state students may have different deadlines than in-state students.

applying
on-line

Web sites provide information as well as downloadable forms, on-line applications, common applications, and multiple submissions. Check these sites in advance to determine which one you'll use:

www.collegelink.com
www.collegeapps.com
www.collegenet.com
www.weapply.com
app.commonapp.org

admission tricks

If you don't need financial aid—let 'em know. If the school is short on funds or loaded with applicants who need aid, it may help.

The 'hot' college that everyone in your class wants to go to will be harder to get accepted. Too many applicants from one school can cut down your chances. If there's a school you want to go to, keep your mouth shut!

Colleges give points for geographical diversity (state and rural/urban), being related to an alumni, and ethnicity. Consider schools in various locations and don't forget schools family members attended.

Wanna let the colleges know you're really interested? Ask for an interview with the admissions officer and talk to the professors in your desired major. You'll stand out as an applicant.

A college is more likely to accept you if your major is in an 'under-enrolled' area. Ask the admissions officer how your choice of major might affect your chances.

Stand out! Colleges give extra points for talent and athletic ability. Let 'em know what you can do.

Don't let your parents do it! YOU make the phone calls to the college for information. You may not be as polished but your enthusiasm and interest count more.

Don't just apply to 'reach' schools. Include at least one 'safety' school in the bunch. You don't want to end up with 6 rejections and no place to go.

Market yourself! If you do something special—art, photography, music, etc.— send a sample of your work.

Feel like the 'real' you can't be presented in a common application? **Submit added information or explanations.** Make sure your social security number and name is on every page.

Call every school you've applied to and **make sure your application has been received and is complete.** If anything is missing, get it to them pronto!

Send thank you note after interviews, visits or if an admissions officer has been extremely helpful. You'll get your name in front of them again.

Didn't make the 'cut' at the college of your choice? Find out what community college that school uses as its 'feeder' school. Do your 2 year core curriculum there and you'll be able to transfer. It's a great way to save money, too.

Apply Early Decision only to your first choice school — applying ED is like adding 100 points to your SAT score.

If you know alumni from the college—a relative, employer, volunteer supervisor —ask them to write a letter of recommendation for you.

how to get
good recommendations

Select teachers who know you well (if you have a choice). It's a nice touch to include a letter from a teacher related to your proposed field of study.

▷ **Give each teacher a copy** of your resume and a personal statement of your goals. Include the colleges you're applying to and why you chose them.

▷ **Remind the teacher** who you are. Include any writings from his/her class or remind him/her of any special projects.

▷ **Include any necessary forms** as well as a stamped, self-addressed envelope. Include the deadline date!

▷ **Ask early. . .** before everyone else does. At the end of junior year, they'll have the summer to write it. Do a polite follow up to make sure the letter was completed and sent.

▷ **Follow instructions.** If a school requests a letter from a language teacher, don't substitute. If they want two letters, don't send three.

▷ **Send thank you notes**—handwritten, no emails!

66 Don't TELL me you 'need' a
recommendation . . .
I'm honored to be ASKED. 99

High School Counselor

early decision

Early Decision is an option offered by some schools. Simply, you apply early and you find out early if you're accepted. Early Decision can lessen your senior year load but it has pitfalls:

▶ **It's binding.** If they accept you, you've got to go to that school. If you apply Early Decsion make sure it's your first choice school.

▶ **You can't compare financial aid** packages. Because you're committed, the school may not feel the need to be generous to you. They'll use the money to entice another student.

▶ **Early Action** works the same way as early decision but it's non-binding. Check to see if your school of choice offers Early Action as well as Early Decision. Weigh your options carefully.

▶ **Don't slack off** on regular applications to other schools.

don't even think about . . .

applying **Early Decision** to more than one

school.Many schools share applicatin lists.

If your name appears on more than one list,

you can be dropped from all of them.

making the
final decision . . .

"A&M had my friends but SWT had the majors I was interested in. It was hard, but I left my friends. It's been a good choice . . . I couldn't be happier."
**Sophomore,
Southwest Texas U.**

66 I always thought I wanted a small school... but my mom made me apply to a large university too. That's where I ended up... I love the environment, the diversity, and all the experiences that go with it. College is more than books. 99

Freshman, U. of Texas

"Don't choose a college to be close to your boyfriend. I fell out of love with him AND the college.
**Freshman,
Converse College**

66 Look at the freshman support services, especially if you're an athlete. You're not going to have the time other kids have to figure out all the new student 'issues.' 99

Sophomore, U. of Texas

> Everyone thinks it's good to go away.
> But I missed home. I missed the place that
> I had hated living in my entire life.
> I came back. It's been a great experience . . .
> college IS what you make it.

Sophomore, U. of Nevada, Reno

"Both of my sisters went here.
I just followed them. I'll always
wonder how happy I could have been
someplace else."
Freshman, Texas A&M

> Take it from a 'transfer,' I learned the hard way .
> . . look for an environment
> with things to do outside of school.

Junior, U. of Minnesota

"Listen to your heart.
Pick a college that fits YOU."
**Sophomore,
U. of Minnesota**

> This school's in a tiny little town in the middle
> of nowhere and it's been the most fabulous
> four years I could imagine. On campus and off,
> everyone feels like 'family.'

Freshman, Murray State U.

"I didn't 'make' a decision.
I just went where my friends went.
It was SO big. I felt SO lost. Great
school—not for me. Marion is a tenth
of the size but it's so 'me'."
Junior, Marion College

have you been
waitlisted?

Being put on the waiting list offers you a ray of hope but **be realistic.** Schools can wait list anywhere from 100 to over 2,000 students, many times with little chance of getting in. If you really want to be accepted, don't just sit there:

▷ **Let 'em know you want in.** Call the admissions department and tell them they're your first choice. Ask what you can do to increase your chances.

▷ **Send extra letters** of recommendation, especially ones that pertain to your field of study or highlight how your being on campus would benefit the college.

▷ **Being 'em up to date.** Get your grades up and tell them. Let them know about any new honors or awards you've received or new involvement in community service and activities.

▷ **Ask for another interview** and razzle dazzle them.

▷ **Let them know** if you don't need financial help. Many times coffers are nearly empty and paying your own way could make a difference.

▷ **Consider the schools** that accepted you. *You're their FIRST choice.*

. . . can't get in fall semester?

Ask about **'multientry admissions'**. In other words, enrolling in spring, winter, or summer? Many colleges are beginning to offer this option to keep seats full.

66 . . . more students should consider
small liberal arts colleges . . .
where endowments are spent on
the pupils themselves,
not supporting 22 Division 1 sports. 99

Seppy Basili, Institute for Academic Excellence,
in *Newsweek's How to Get into College 1999*

vacancies...

The National Association of College Admission
counselors' (NACAC) web site posts colleges that have
openings for their freshman class AFTER the May 1
deadline. Hop onto the site and click onto the 'Space
Availability'. Survey for state-by-state listings of colleges
you can still apply to: **www.nacac.com**

deferred admissions

Many colleges allow students who have been accepted to
take up to a year off before starting classes. Deferred
admissions are granted to allow you to work full time,
clarify your career goals, travel or volunteer. You won't be
allowed to take classes for credit during that time but,
depending on your travel or volunteer work, you may be
awarded credit hours. Each school's policy is different, so
check with your admissions officer **before** you apply.

66 If there's something that would tell us
more about you, include it with your application.
It does make a difference—especially if you're
borderline for admission. 99

Admissions Officer, Michigan State U.

options...

the 'CC' edge

There are definite advantages to starting your college career at a Community College. They offer a lot of flexibility in terms of time, money, and the type of degree you can obtain—two year associate degrees, certification, **or simply** taking core classes closer to home.

▷ **Yearly tuition at a CC is less** than $2,000, half the cost of a 4 year public college, and only a tenth of the cost of a 4 year private college. Do your core curriculum at a CC and you'll save up to 50% on your bachelor's degree. Plus, you're still eligible for scholarships and federal grants and loans.

▷ **SATs and ACTs are not considered.** You will need a high school diploma, its equivalency and/or pass a high school 'exit' exam.

▷ **Classes are offered at various times** during the day, evenings, and weekends, and many have online courses—a plus if you want or need to work.

> 66 Get rid of a course you're dreading
> by taking it at a community college
> during the summer
> before classes start.
> I wish I had . . . my math course
> sucked up so much time
> during the first semester
> that I got crummy grades
> in everything. 99

Junior, Southern Illinois U.
from Been There Should've Done That

> **"** Your first day of class
> is the first day of your career.
> You better be prepared to 'own' this...
> otherwise you'll drown. **"**

Admissions Couselor, Full Sail

the fast track

Do you have a passion? If you know exactly what you want to do with the rest of your life and you're in a hurry, there may be a school out there just for you. BUT, **forget football games, fraternities, and cutting class**—these 'no-nonsense' programs are intense, accelerated and *professional.*

▶ **Every course you take** will be related to the field or industry that you intend as your career. If you're in Video Production, your math will include such things as figuring the wattage necessary to light a movie set. If you're in Video Game Programming, your English may include developing a promotional package for a new game or writing a review. Sociology will consist of analyzing how technology effects the world.

▶ **It can be fast**—12 months to 4 years, depending on the type of degree or certification necessary to complete the program.

▶ **You are 'plugged in'** to your field—to the latest trends and technology—as well as job contacts.

for accredited . . .

career schools go to:

_____

www.accsct.org

the short list...
career schools

3-D Animation	Film
Architectural Drafting	Golf
Art	Graphic Design
Aviation	Hospitality Management
Broadcasting	Interior Design
Business	Legal Administration
Computer Aided Drafting	Nursing
Computer Information Systems	Personal Trainer
Culinary Arts	Photography
Dental Hygiene	Recording Arts
Digital Media	Show Production
Fashion Design	Turf Management
	Video Game Design

For more information, apptitude tests, a discussion of your options and links to schools:

www.degreestosucceed.com

www.computer-schools.info

www.search4business-schools.com

www.techdegree.net

www.collegelookup.com

university of internet...

You can get a degree on-line—or just take a few classes. But it takes a lot of discipline! Finding an on-line school isn't difficult but make sure the school is accreditied. Get more information and check out what's available at: **www.classesusa.com** or **www.online-college-dgree.com**

applying

Deadlines will vary from school to school. Keep your eye on due dates.

Fall:

☐ **Narrow down** your college choices and create a file for each college's information.

☐ **Create** a calendar of deadlines for each college. Then create a master calendar for all deadlines.

☐ **Make** sure you know who's responsible for gathering the necessary information (transcripts and records) and submitting your application, or if it's totally up to you. **(Be a control freak. Even if your high school does take care of this process, check with the guidance office frequently to make sure deadlines are being met.)**

☐ **Be** sure your final SAT/ACT scores have been sent to your selected colleges.

☐ **Decide** if you want to apply Early Decision or Early Action. Remember, these deadlines will be earlier.

☐ **Ask** your teachers, counselors and/or coaches for recommendations (page 122).

☐ **Download** or send for your college applications after August 1 at the colleges' web sites or check the application help sites (page 119). Get applications for housing and financial aid at the same time.

☐ **Make copies** of all blank applications (financial ones, too). Use the copies to make rough drafts. Follow each school's directions to the letter.

☐ **Finish** all required essays.

☐ **Verify** your high school transcript. Order official transcripts to be sent directly to each college on your list.

☐ **Make copies** of each completed application for your files.

☐ **Turn in** your applications to your counselor. (Check that they've been mailed in time to meet your deadlines.)

☐ **Check** that recommendations from teachers have been sent to the college or forwarded to your counselor for her to send to the college.

☐ **Call** the admissions offices of your colleges at least once to verify your application is complete and nothing is missing. If anything is missing, get it to them immediately.

Winter:

☐ **Withdraw** your other college applications immediately if you are accepted Early Decision.

☐ **Begin** the financial aid process (page 135).

Spring:

☐ **Check** housing deadlines, deposits and refund procedures. Make deposits where necessary to put a hold on dorm space. If you haven't decided which college to attend yet, only send in those deposits that are refundable.

☐ **Review** and compare acceptance and financial aid award letters (page 138).

☐ **Choose** your college and notify the schools you won't be attending. You must do this to free up space for another student.

☐ **Call** the admissions officer if you are waitlisted. Ask how you can improve your application or better your chances.

☐ **Send** in your enrollment deposit.

☐ **Verify** your housing situation with your college. Apply for housing deposit refunds from the colleges you won't be attending.

☐ **Make** your reservation for orientation and registration (page 145).

☐ **Give** a copy of your acceptance letter to your counselor for your file.

☐ **Send** thank you notes to everyone who has helped you. Inform them what school you'll be attending. Don't forget to include the staff in the guidance office!

'Senioritis'
is NOT your new Spanish teacher

66 I just felt like I didn't need
any more hard work!
The worst part was that
it continued into my
first semester at college . . .
not a good thing. 99

Sophomore, Cornell U.

66 If you're thinking about dropping
academic classes listed
on your application, think again.
Colleges DO
review your senior records. 99

High School Counselor

Senioritis: (n., se'-ne-or-i-tis; from the latin meaning "time to party") A condition that affects 12th graders who believe they can coast through the last year of high school. Symptoms include falling GPAs, lower class rank, missed opportunities to lessen freshman college load. Rare cases have resulted in grades so low, accepting colleges have reversed their decision. **Prescribed cure:** continued reality checks and acting in one's own best interest.

money 102

. . . getting it.

Financial aid is a 'first come, first served' operation. Wait too long to send in your forms and the coffers will be empty. So, get your applications in as soon as the process will allow. **For FAFSA, that means beginning January 1.** Since FAFSA relies on numbers from your parents' 1040 income tax form, you'll want your parents to complete their return quickly (although they don't have to file them until April 15). Get your tax return done quickly, too. **The CSS/Profile must be filed at least four weeks before your college's 'priority filing date'.**

the forms . . . .

fafsa

(for basic information on FAFSA and the financial aid process, see Money 101, page 91)

FAFSA is the federal form for student aid. It's available from your high school counselor or at your guidance office. You can get a paper application by calling 1-800-4FEDAID, or apply for FAFSA on line at:

www.fafsa.ed.gov

Even if you think you won't be eligible for need-based aid, fill out the FAFSA. You won't be able to get federally-backed loans (which come at a much lower rate) without filing it.

the fafsa pin...

If you decide to complete the FAFSA on-line, register for a PIN (Personal Identification Number) at least a month before. Without a PIN, you'll have to print the signature page and snail mail it. Get your PIN at: **www.pin.ed.gov**

why file on-line?

Filing your FAFSA on-line gets your Student Aid Report (SAR) to you at least two weeks faster. Electronically filing your CSS/Profile gets it to the schools and scholarships at least 5 days sooner—a huge advantage when being first in line can get you a sweeter financial aid package. **The big bonus is that applications are automatically checked before being processed.** When you hit the 'submit' button, your form is scanned before being sent. You'll know of an omissions or incorrectly-entered data immediately. That could save you weeks of time correcting errors.

css/profile

Over 600 schools and scholarships require the Profile offered by the College Board. Each school has its own 'priority' filing date. **You must register for the Profile at least 4 weeks before the schools priority filing date.** Profile forms are available through your high school counselor, by calling College Board at 1-800-778-6888 or you can file it electronically. But, once you register for the paper application you CANNOT switch to the on-line version. Visit the web site for instructions and tips on filing the Profile before you register. To file on the Internet go to: **www.collegeboard.com**

special applications...

Some colleges, especially the more selective ones, have their own financial form in addition to the FAFSA or Profile. Call the college's financial aid department to find out what forms are needed, the deadlines, and to request any special application.

don't NOT do it!

Thinking of NOT filling out the FAFSA form? You'll hurt yourself in more ways than one:

- Some scholarships and grants will disqualify you if you haven't sent in FAFSA.
- Many student employment situations won't consider you unless you apply for aid—even if you believe you won't qualify.

comparing aid packages...

Two financial aid offers of $13,000—are they equal?
Not if one is mostly grants and the other mostly
loans. Before you accept—or reject— any offers,
use the 'Compare Aid Award' tools at:
www.collegeboard.com

yes, you can appeal a financial aid package

Didn't get enough aid from your first choice school? Did
another school offer a better aid package? Before you write
off a school or remortgage the house, ask the financial aid
officer to reconsider the aid package.

▶ **Explain that the school is your first choice** but
another school has made a better offer (if that's
the case).

▶ **If there are extenuating family circumstances**
(medical bills, divorce, loss of a job), explain them.

▶ **Don't lie.** The FAO will want supporting evidence
for any claim you make, including a copy of the
other school's aid package.

. . . when student aid, isn't

PLUS Loans should never be included in a
school's financial aid offer. PLUS Loans—
federally backed loans to parents—are
designed to help parents deal with their
EFC and any unmet need.

> 66 Check out your state schools,
> especially for financial help.
> Nevada high school grads
> get a $10,000 scholarship to go to
> Nevada state colleges. That helps! 99

Freshman, U. of Nevada

'FinAid' tips

Don't wait to get an acceptance letter to apply for aid. By that time, most of the aid will be gone.

College financial aid deadlines are different—and usually earlier—than federal and state deadlines. Miss a college deadline and you may only qualify for loans.

Early Decision could mean early deadlines. Check with the financial aid officer for deadline dates.

Even if you don't qualify for federal aid, you may qualify for state aid. States are more generous than the federal government.

Watch those scholarship deadlines and requirements. **Missing one or having an incomplete application will jeopardize your eligibility— even if it's not your fault.**

Empty spaces on your financial aid forms will count as errors and cause delays. Enter '0' in lines that don`t apply.

Call the financial aid offices to confirm your application has been received and is complete. If something is missing, get it to them quickly.

Correct errors immediately. Errors slow down the process which can ultimately limit your aid.

Keep copies of EVERYTHING! You'll need them if your forms get lost or to correct errors.

Ask your parents to call the Human Resources Department where they work and **ask if the company will pay any of the tuition for employee's children.**

R.O.T.C.
atten-shun!

▷ **The ROTC provides scholarships** at about 600 schools nationwide. In exchange for active duty or part-time duty in the National Guard or Reserves after you graduate, you'll get the vast majority of your tuition paid PLUS a graduated living stipend of $200 - $350 a month.

▷ **Enlist in any of the service branches** after you graduate and Uncle Sam will help pay off that student loan.

▷ **If you parents are or were in the service**, loan assistance is also available.

For information on all the ways the military can help you, go to:

www.students.gov

one more fafsa tip...

All males must register with Selective Service by their 18th birthday. Not registering will disqualify you from receiving federal aid. You can register on the FAFSA form or, go to:

www.sss.gov

money 102

If you are applying Early Decision or Early Action your timeline may be early also. Make adjustments.

August/September:

☐ **Request** any special financial aid forms your college may use in addition to the CSS Profile and FAFSA.

☐ **Create** a calendar of all financial aid and scholarship deadlines.

☐ **Check** with your state's Department of Education for state aid applications and deadlines. Or, access them at:

www.students.gov

☐ **Download** or send for scholarship applications. Make note of their deadlines.

☐ **Attend** financial aid workshops provided by your high school or colleges.

☐ **Ask** for teacher recommendations for scholarships, if you didn't do it last spring.

September/October:

☐ **Register and complete** the CSS/Profile, one month before a school's priority filing date if the school requires it. Call or register on-line (page 137).

December:

☐ **Apply** for a FAFSA PIN at:

www.pin.ed.gov.

☐ **Get** a copy of FAFSA, available from your high school counselor, direct from the government by calling 1-800-4FEDAID, or download a copy at:

www.fafsa.ed.gov

January:

☐ **Have** your parents complete their income tax form 1040 as soon as possible. Get your tax form completed.

☐ **Complete** FAFSA and send it in quickly.

☐ **Make** a copy of all financial aid forms.

February:

☐ **Call** the schools' financial aid offices to confirm your application has been received and is complete.

☐ **Make** sure your scholarship applications are complete and requirements met.

☐ **Go over** your SAR (Student Aid Report) for errors. Correct any errors immediately.

March/April:

☐ **Send** copies of your tax forms and SAR to financial officers, **if requested.**

☐ **Compare** financial aid packages. Use a tuition calculator (page 138) to compare offers.

☐ **Determine** whether you want to appeal your aid package (page 138).

☐ **Make** your final decision. Sign and return the required forms promptly.

☐ **Inform** the financial aid offices of the schools you won't be attending. This is necessary to free up money for other students.

May:

☐ **Ask** the financial aid counselor if the school participates in a direct lending program for student/parent loans. If they do, request applications and return them completed. Also ask if you can file the applications on-line to save time.

☐ **Contact** local banks and lenders if the school does not participate in direct lending. Be specific and request information on federally-backed student loans.

Summer:

☐ **Make money!** Save money!

☐ **Apply now** for a job in the fall, particularly if your financial aid package includes work study. The 'good' jobs go fast—particularly on campus.

☐ **Start looking** for scholarships for next year!

66 The best thing
my parents did for me
was have their taxes done
by February 2nd every year. 99

Senior, Milwaukee School of Engineering

. . . congratulations!

Your hard work has paid off! But as your high school career winds down and you have one foot out the door, there are still a few things you can do now and through the summer to make your life easier as a college freshman. Your most important assignment: read, study, and scrutinize everything your new school sends you. Along with the necessary forms and deadlines, you'll be notified of all kinds of special freshman programs and opportunities that can make your transition to college a piece of cake. **Take advantage of them.**

you're in!

Spring:

☐ **Watch** the deadlines for deposits!

☐ **Fill out** necessary forms and return them promptly (housing, roommate profile, medical, etc.). Waiting may affect whether you get into any special programs, your choice of dorms — or even whether you will be able to live in the dorms.

☐ **Read** carefully whatever material is sent to you about freshman programs, activities, and opportunities. You may also check wth the college's web site for a list or call the Department of New Student Services.

☐ **Register** for the earliest orientation session as soon as you're accepted. That should improve your chances of getting the classes you want.

☐ **Request** your housing deposits back from the college(s) you're not attending. If you miss the deadline your money will not be refunded.

☐ **Consider** taking courses at a community college or on your prospective campus during the summer. It's a chance to learn a skill (i.e. time management, computers), brush up on a weak area (i.e. math) or simply get a class out of the way. Find out whether the credits transfer.

☐ **Make sure** that your final transcript is sent to your college.

☐ **Look** for a summer job.

Summer:

- ☐ **Notify** your college of any scholarships you've received.

- ☐ **Peruse** the college's web site for tips on orientation, registration and information in general. Read the discussion boards and chat sites to get 'inside' advice and meet students.

- ☐ **Contact** your roommate. Get acquainted via phone or e-mail and decide who's bringing what. Dorm rooms are small.

- ☐ **Make a list** of PINS, credit card numbers, registration numbers, and leave them at home where you'll know where to find them. Also, list the serial numbers on computers, printers, bicycles or anything else that may be stolen, so that there's no problem with insurance.

- ☐ **Read**. Get a list of titles you'll have to read as a freshman and dig in (page 33).

❝ I felt like a juggler trying to keep all the plates spinning because I couldn't decide which college to go to. We had to fill out forms and keep on top of deadlines for all of them. ❞

Freshman, DePaul U.

make the most
of orientation

If you're on campus for orientation it's a good time to 'take care of business'. If your school doesn't have a summer orientation, plan a visit anyway so you can:

▷ **Meet with a Financial Aid Officer.** Summers are a lot more laid back so you'll be able to get advice specific to your circumstances and give him a chance to connect a face with the financial forms... could benefit you in the future.

▷ **Find a work study job** if you're responsible for securing one.

▷ **Contact any club**, organization, or activity your interested in. You may be able to jump in sooner and beat the rush for prime positions in the fall.

▷ **Scan the newspaper** and bulletin boards for lofts, refrigerators, used books, parking spaces, or whatever.

. . . make your life easier

Read the course description catalog BEFORE
orientation. Make a list of courses that interest
you so you'll have alternatives if you can't get
your 1st choice. . .there's a good chance
you won't.

too good to miss!

You need to know that colleges spend big dollars on programs to help freshmen succeed . . . **but you have to enroll in them!**

Freshman Seminars—Learning Communities—Residential Colleges—FIG's (Freshman Interest Groups)—Mentoring . . .whatever your college calls it, these programs are specifically designed to provide you with a built-in support system of students, faculty and advisers. They allow excellent on-going access to faculty and advisers, and allow you to find your 'niche' academically and socially. Space is usually limited, **so register early.**

Pre-orientation programs. These programs are meant to be nothing more than FUN—an opportunity to bond with fellow freshmen. The activities include such things as wilderness trips, white-water rafting, service projects, retreats, etc. Take a bit of time from your 'last summer' with friends and ease into meeting new ones. Again, space is usually limited so **register early.**

doctor, doctor...

- **Get a physical** in early spring. Schedule vaccinations for: Hepatitus B (3 doses—start in May), Meningitis and Tetanus (if due).
- **Make a list** of your allergies to give to your dorm advisor, especially if you're allergic to medications.
- **Transfer any prescriptions** to a pharmacy near your college.

sticker shock

The first semester can be a quite a surprise for unsuspecting freshmen and their parents.
Prepare yourself for 'add-on' fees.
Here's the 'real thing'. . .

Payment Due: December 12, 2

On-line Correspondence:
fbic@forum.utexas.edu

http://www.utexas.edu/bus

Payable to:
niversity of Texas at Austin

Send Correspondence to:
Main Building Room 4
24th & Guadalupe Street
Austin, Texas 78705
(512) 475-7777

ments to:
versity of Texas at Austin
x 13177
, Texas 78711-3177

ERCE, ASHLIE DENISE

Description	Total	Charges
TUITION & FEES		1,176.00
TUITION - 14 HOURS		601.16
FEES REQ OF ALL STUDENTS		122.00
ADVISING FEE-BUSINESS UG		155.00
PLACEMENT FEE - BUS UG		190.00
INSTRUCT TECH FEE-BUS UG		2.00
DOLLARS FOR SCHOLARS		282.00
COURSE RELATED FEES	2,528.16	
CURRENT BALANCE	2,528.16	

*the 'extra's'

Fees required of all students	601.16
Advising Fee-Business UG	122.00
Placement Fee-Bus UG	155.00
Instruct Tech Fee-Bus UG	190.00
Dollars For Scholars	2.00
Course Related Fees	202.00
	$1272.16

*first semester

dollars & sense

setting up your finances

Along with learning how to say, "Do you give a student discount?" it's time to set up your financial life and familiarize yourself with banking. Talk to your parents now to find out what they expect of you. Have them define what a 'financial emergency' is (hint: it probably won't be new designer clothes for 'rush week') and how it should be handled. Asking them for tips on how to budget your money isn't a bad idea either.

bank that

Sit down with your parents in early summer and set up your finances:

▷ **Look for a bank** with a branch office in your college town if you're in the same state. Or, open a checking account with the college's business office.

▷ **Ask the bank** what the procedures are for interstate banking if your school is in a different state. (You'll want your parents to be able to deposit funds for you.)

▷ **Give an adequate supply of deposit slips** to your parents if they don't have direct access to your bank.

▷ **Activate an on-line account** if your bank offers that service.

▷ **Get a credit/debit card** to use in emergencies. (have your parents define 'emergency').

▷ **Learn how to balance** your checking account and how to read a bank statement.

▷ **Ask if the college provides** information about budgeting, credit cards and money management.

▷ **Find out where the fee-free** ATMs are on campus.

▷ **Learn how to ask** "Do you give a student discount?" Many stores will give you one even if it isn't their policy.

. . . super saver

Able to pay your tuition in one lump sum?

Great!

Ask the college if they'll give you a discount.

credit or debit?
the case for/against

Debit Cards:

A great alternative to carrying cash and a safe way to learn about credit without high interest charges. A must-have for the 'self-control-challenged' student.

Going over your balance causes overdraft fees. There's overdraft protection but it has a high interest. No protection if someone steals your card—they've got your cash. Does not build credit history.

Credit Cards:

Can't be beat for real emergencies and if you're responsible, you can build a great credit history. Most cards are theft-protected (if stolen, you don't pay for charges). Look for a card that gives you something back: frequent flyer miles, cash back, and/or purchase protection.

Don't pay off your balance every month and the interest rates will send that balance soaring. There's a chance of graduating with a student loan AND a credit debt. The real nasty: your future employers check your credit rating.

To find and compare credit cards, go to:

www.studentmarket.com

insurance
basics

Your possessions should be covered by your parents' home-owners' policy IF you're living in a dorm. If you're living off-campus or planning to move off-campus in your later college years, you'll need your own renter's insurance.

Check to see if there's enough specific coverage on your current homeowners' policy for items such as your computer and jewelry, too. A $1,000 worth of electronic coverage may not be enough if it has to cover both your computer and CD player AND your parents' electronic items. If you have any doubts, talk to your insurance agent about purchasing an additional rider'.

Find out if you will still be covered by your parents' car insurance if you're taking your car with you.

Don't forget health insurance. If your parents can't cover you, check with the college for medical and dental policies they may offer.

dollars & sense

☐ **Talk** with your parents. Find out what they will pay for and what you'll be responsible for once you're on campus.

☐ **Check** to see if the college has a 'student savings account' where your parents can deposit cash for your withdrawl.

☐ **Set up** your banking. Open a checking or savings account and ATM card on campus..

☐ **Decide** on either a debit or credit cards. If you want a credit card, research your options thoroughly for the best rates and benefits.

☐ **Practice** writing checks, balancing your account and using an ATM before you get on campus.

☐ **Get** a taste of reality. Find out what the charges are for a bounced check or an overdraft on a debit card now. If you know what it costs, you'll be less likely to do it.

☐ **Review** your insurance needs. Ask your parents to check their homeowners' policy to see if your possessions are adequately covered, especially for computers and jewelry. Call your insurance agent if you have any doubt.

☐ **Budget** in extra money for trips home, mass transportation, gas, haircuts, manicures, clothes, and dry cleaning.

☐ **Make** a list of all your PINs (and registration numbers) to leave at home. If you lose a number, you'll know where a safe copy is.

and etc. . . .

. . . getting ready

Picking out all the things you'll need for your dorm is cool . . . until you realize how all those odds and ends can nickel and dime you to death. Plan ahead, shop wisely and you may even have enough money left over to buy yourself lunch.

66 It's horrible to buy toothpaste, shampoo and toilet paper with your own money. 99

Freshman, Texas A&M

computer
basics

Before you buy a computer check with your college for their specs. Once you have those requirements, turn your attention to getting as much speed, RAM and storage as you can afford. Then there's only 3 things you have to decide:

▸ **Desk top or Laptop:** Desk tops do take up more room but laptops have drawbacks. They're easier to steal and they get knocked around which can cause bad sectors which can ultimately ruin a hard drive. Upgrading them is difficult if not impossible. And a small keyboard contributes to repetitive motion injury. While you can't beat their portability, the extra dollars they cost could be used to buy a more powerful desktop.

▸ **PC or MAC:** What are you used to using and what will you need? PCs are less expensive than MACs but depending on your major—graphic arts, for example—you may need a MAC. If you're not sure what you need, call your academic advisor or check with the department of your major.

▸ **Printer?** Considering how inexpensive they are, yes. Colleges allow you to use their printers but once you use the pages allowed or want a color printout, you pay.

66 I get music, movies, and can talk to my friends for free. TVs, phones, even a car isn't as necessary as a computer. **99**

Freshman, U. of Texas

phone
phacts

Regular phone, cell phone or both? After you check with your college to see what service they offer, shop around. There are ways to cut down on your bill with a little restraint and a few tricks:

▶ **Use calling cards for long-distance.** Watch for local store sales and shop for good rates.

▶ **Ask your parents to get an '800' number.** It's much cheaper than collect calls from you.

▶ **Don't be swayed by free cell phones,** free activation, or initial low rates. And don't listen to sales people. Read the entire contract—fine print, too.

▶ **Don't use cell phone minutes** for ordering pizza or calling radio station give-aways—you're wasting your minutes.

▶ **Use e-mail or Instant Messaging whenever possible.**

▶ **Incoming cell calls cost YOU.** If you get too many, get a pager. You can choose who and when to call back.

▶ **Don't make all of your calls during peak hours** if your plan divides the time between peak and off hours.

▶ **Some cell phone plans charge for dialing '800'** numbers. Check before you sign the contract.

what you'll need

Linens:
- 2 sets of twin sheets (long)
- Blankets or quilts
- Pillows
- Mattress pad (long)

Bath:
- Shower shoes, caddie
- Towels
- Soap, shampoo, conditioner
- Toothbrush, paste
- Hairbrush, comb, hairdryer

Desk:
- Stationery (include stamps)
- Calculator
- Calendar, planner
- Bulletin board
- Lap desk

Furniture:
- Full length mirror
- Fold up stools, butterfly chairs, or floor pillows
- Waste basket
- CD player

Storage:
- Bed lifters (creates storage area under bed)
- Storage boxes
- Milk crates, shelves
- Over-the-door rack

Other:
- Lamps, flashlight, batteries
- Sewing kit
- Iron, ironing board
- Dishes, silverware
- Food storage containers
- Wall-friendly poster tape
- Extension cords, surge protectors
- Tool set
- Alarm Clock
- Hangers
- First aid kit
- Ear plugs

To be decided with roommate:
- Refrigerator/cooler
- Microwave
- Vacuum
- TV

66 Take BLEACH,
you don't think you need it
until you do. . . germs happen 99

Sophomore, Western Michigan U.

to etc. do's

- [ ] **Check** with your college for their computer hardware and software specs.

- [ ] **Find out** if your major dictates what type of computer you need. Find out if your college offers a computer sales program for students. Colleges that have this program usually sell at not-for-profit prices.

- [ ] **Factor** in tech support when buying a computer. You'll want it available around the clock.

- [ ] **Upgrade** your current computer with more speed if you plan to take it with you.

- [ ] **Make** sure you have adequate insurance and warranty coverage for your computer.

- [ ] **Make** a list of your computer's serial, model and registration numbers to leave at home for safekeeping.

- [ ] **Check** with your college for the type of phone service available. Compare their rates to cell phones to find the least expensive deal.

- [ ] **Ask** your parents to add an '800' number to their present phone service.

☐ **Stock up** on calling cards when you find a good rate. Drop hints to your relatives that phone cards make great gifts.

☐ **Contact** your college's Office of Residential Life for a list of restricted items before you shop for your dorm decor.